IMAGES
of America

PROMISED LAND STATE PARK

Alden Whitman once wrote, "Our ideals, laws, and customs should be based on the proposition that each generation in turn becomes the custodian rather than the absolute owner of our resources, and each generation has the obligation to pass this inheritance on to the future." And so it is with Promised Land State Park—it is everyones duty to pass those resources on to their children and grandchildren and their children. (Courtesy Herbert Witzenberger.)

On the cover: see page 23. (Courtesy Pennsylvania State Archives.)

IMAGES
of America

PROMISED LAND STATE PARK

Peter Osborne

ARCADIA
PUBLISHING

ISBN 978-0-7385-3865-5

Published by Arcadia Publishing
Charleston, South Carolina

Printed in the United States of America

Library of Congress Control Number: 2005926065

For all general information, please contact Arcadia Publishing:
Telephone 843-853-2070
Fax 843-853-0044
E-mail sales@arcadiapublishing.com
For customer service and orders:
Toll-Free 1-888-313-2665

Visit us on the Internet at www.arcadiapublishing.com

To my wife, Janis; Ryan; Megan; Beth; Gary; Lauren; Rachel; G. P.; Kerrie; Meaghan; Christina; Mary; Steve; Steve Jr.; Andrew; and my mother, Barbara.

Contents

Acknowledgments 6

Introduction 7

1. The Promised Land 9
2. A Grand Vision 25
3. We Can Take It! The Arrival of the Civilian Conservation Corps 39
4. The Civilian Conservation Corps Work Projects at Promised Land State Park 59
5. The People's Park 83
6. Promised Land State Park Today 99
7. Looking To The Future 111

Bibliography 128

ACKNOWLEDGMENTS

Without the following people, institutions, and agencies I could not have completed this work. I acknowledge the work of several individuals who have contributed to the park's history. First is former park superintendent Sanford Shelton, who played an important role in the creation of this book by having written, along with his wife Wendy Anne Riblett, several histories of the park. Their work was the basis on which I began. The second, Peg Bancroft, has written about the area's history and offered suggestions and photographs. Finally, Evelyn Wilson Haldaman has been collecting materials about the park's history and the Wilson family association with the park for many years.

I am indebted to Barbara Davey, the former park manager, for her support and Leo Davidovich, current park manager, who was always helpful. Bill Wasser, assistant park manager, and Jen Naugle, environmental education specialist, discussed at length the park's history and operations. Richard "the Pavilion Man" Demi, Debbie Wells, Christy Loomis, Sheri Dalrymple, and Sarah Chapel all get gold stars for their help in light of my many requests during my time at Promised Land. Collectively, the park's staff, past and present, provides a good example of how to manage a wonderful park operation.

Various commonwealth agencies provided information, including Pennsylvania Geologic Survey; Jon Inners, Department of Conservation and Natural Resources; Rodger Cook and his staff at the Land Records Section, Division of Field Engineering; James J. McElwee; Joe Maculaitis; Bill Delling; John Bitzer; and the Pennsylvania State Archives and the Pennsylvania Historical and Museum Commission, both in Harrisburg.

Friends and supporters of the park who assisted include Tom Frantz; Keith Kleckner; Jean Zane; Kathleen Sharp; William Douglass; William Clark; Richard Gassmann; Margaret Weitz Hunter; Jack Cressman; Sandi Naughton; Donald Heiney; Robert Koehler; Lester Christman; George Fluhr; Dr. Mead Shaffer; Geoffrey Gross; Kathy Mason; the New York State Historical Association; Kurt Reed, local glass expert and historian; Hank Loftus, curator-program director of the Dorflinger-Suydam Wildlife Sanctuary at White Mills; Harry Leitheiser; Greene Township Historical Society; Robert Hazelton; Herbert Witzenberger; the Philadelphia Water Department; Adam Levine; Drew Brown; Ed Grusheski; Congressman Donald Sherwood and his staff; Sandra Wescoe; Evelyn and Al Haldaman; Wallenpaupack Historical Society; Jon Tandy; Clayton Price; Alisa Price; Carl Rose; Erwin Weber; the family of Francis Leo Bowerman; Virginia Wells; Beverly Puhl; Len and Lucille Martin; Paul Nauman; Moriah Newnam; Peggy Newnam; Bill Davies; Betty Thompson; Florence Gray; Betty Collins; Jerry Grant, director of research and library services; and Sharon Koomler, director of the Shaker Museum and Library, Old Chatham, New York, extended professional courtesies. Many area residents, campers, visitors, and park advocates provided information about the park.

I am grateful to Nancy Conod and Nancy Vocci, the Minisink Valley Historical Society's best researchers, for helping with many research requests, reading the manuscript, and offering advice. Lynn and Ernie Bush provided insight about the park's history, and David Heiney took many of the photographs. While all of the people listed helped me immensely with this project, any mistakes contained in this book are mine.

INTRODUCTION

This is a book about three important developments in the history of Pennsylvania's forests and parks: first, the creation and history of one of its most popular state parks, Promised Land State Park; second, the largest national conservation movement ever undertaken in the United States; and third, the postwar vision of creating a state park system that would serve every Pennsylvanian.

The creation of Promised Land State Park is an early example of a larger national movement from 1900–1940 that has been called the Golden Age of Parks. It was a time when many local, county, state, and national parks and forests were established and developed all across the country. The early 1900s witnessed several other major trends that were unfolding as Americans yearned for open spaces with the increased urbanization that was taking place across the land. Automobiles were becoming available to the average American, and as a result, Americans began a great love affair with the road, the automobile, and tent camping. The Boy Scout and Girl Scout movements, established in 1910 and 1912 respectively, blossomed and needed places to conduct outdoor programs. During this era, both organizations grew rapidly and flourished.

In Pennsylvania, other issues were at work as well. Concern for public water supplies, efforts to prevent further destruction of the commonwealth's forests, the needed restoration of the forests, the desire to set aside hundreds of thousands of acres of land for recreational use, the need for wildlife rejuvenation, and the drive to preserve scenic beauty all guided state leaders.

The second development was the important conservation work undertaken by the Civilian Conservation Corps (CCC). It was unprecedented in scope and has never been duplicated in the nation since. From 1933 to 1941, more than 1,800 young men worked at Promised Land in the Depression-era federal agency known as the CCC. It was the brainchild of one of the 20th century's leading figures, Pres. Franklin Delano Roosevelt. The agency had two goals: to give jobs to unemployed young men (between the ages of 17 and 24) and veterans of World War I, and to undertake thousands of conservation projects across the nation in parks, forests, and historic sites.

When the CCC boys arrived at Promised Land in 1933, they found a large, relatively undeveloped tract of land. By the time the CCC boys were finished working eight years later, they had built or enhanced the present-day road systems; planted thousands of trees; built campsites, pavilions, comfort stations, cabins, visitor amenities, trail systems, and Egypt Meadow Lake; and had developed major public access areas that still remain today. The work of the CCC remains the single greatest conservation effort ever undertaken at Promised Land. Some of the projects are gone; however, much of the park enjoyed today is the direct result of their efforts.

The third development, the enhancement of the park as it is known today, was the result of a visionary man, Dr. Maurice Goddard, the secretary of Pennsylvania's Department of Forests and Waters. Goddard was the creator of the Project 70 and Project 500 programs, which essentially built the modern Pennsylvania park system.

Today, on average, more than 400,000 visitors come to the park annually. Promised Land is a jewel in the crown of the state park system, particularly for the region's residents. The park has continued with its mission, maintained the historical integrity of park structures where possible, and regularly expanded and upgraded its facilities. For purposes of clarity, when the author uses the term Promised Land he is referring to the park and not the greater Promised Land region.

As we celebrate the centennial of the park's creation, we remember the many people, agencies, and institutions that have brought us to this point. We acknowledge the people of Pennsylvania who provide the funding for the operation of the commonwealth's parks and forests. We remember the many men and women of the Department of Conservation and Natural Resources and its predecessor agencies who have worked at the park over the years (too numerous to mention) and whose hard work has maintained and preserved the park for the people.

We tip our hats to Pres. Franklin Roosevelt, Gov. Gifford Pinchot, the federal agencies that coordinated the effort of the CCC, and the hard work and dedication of the CCC boys. As you read this book, you will also see that the need for a program similar to the CCC still exists, not only for the benefit of our youth, but for our parks and forests that need the loving care, maintenance, and nurturing the CCC gave them over 60 years ago. Also, we recognize the members of the Youth Conservation Corps, Young Adult Conservation Corps, and the Pennsylvania Conservation Corps who have worked at the park.

Finally, we recognize the friends of the park—long-time visitors, area residents, cabin owners, volunteers, museum donors, campers, local business people, and civic organizations who have a great passion for the park. They have a vested interest in seeing that the park is maintained and its history preserved, and most importantly, they love the place known as Promised Land. In some cases, they have done so for three, four, and five generations.

As we look to the next 100 years, we also recognize the challenges facing the park. The single most critical issue facing Promised Land, like all of the state's parks and forests, is the need for continued public support. One of the purposes of this book is to encourage our elected officials and government leaders to fund our parks and forests in an adequate fashion and to impress upon these leaders the importance of these lands to the people of Pennsylvania. As we look to the park's future, we are hopeful; five generations of visitors have enjoyed this unique place with a name that evokes an optimistic future. As Pennsylvania's Gov. William Stone once said, "The state's parks and forests are, after all, the people's parks and forests."

—Peter Osborne
Executive Director
Minisink Valley Historical Society
Port Jervis, New York

One

THE PROMISED LAND

It is a name that evokes biblical verse and a land of milk and honey. It is also a name whose origin is still debated. One regional historian believes that Promised Land was named by Elias Murray, who helped build the dam that created the original Promised Land Pond. Others have proposed that the name may have come from an early resident who may have been promised land for helping to log off timber, or a promise to Native Americans if they worked at a local sawmill. It has been thought that a religious sect, the Shakers, gave the property its name. Today young visitors may think it is named for the PAX television show called *Promised Land*, in which a family travels in search of the American dream. The earliest citation for the name comes from the park's abstract of title in 1853, when the land around the sawmill pond that later became Promised Land Lake was called the "Promised Land property." The name begins to appear regularly on maps in the late 19th century.

In the 19th century, the extraction of natural resources defined the property. Industries that harvested timber, bark, ice, and bluestone all operated in or near the park. Resources taken from the park and other parts of Pike County found their way across the country and around the world. Today Promised Land is a place of natural beauty, but it was very different in the 19th century.

The park's rugged and rocky landscape is a result of glacial action that passed through the area some 21,000 years ago. When the last glacier melted between 15,000 and 18,000 years ago, tons of glacial till was left behind. Bruce Lake was created by till that dammed the southern end of a swamp and which was fed by springs. Glacial striations can still be seen at the northern end of the lake. (Courtesy Pennsylvania Geological Survey.)

Promised Land sits atop the Pocono Plateau and is located in the western corner of Pike County, Pennsylvania, in parts of Greene, Palmyra, and Blooming Grove townships. Its highest elevation is 1,881 feet, not far from the present-day park office. The east branch of the Wallenpaupack Creek, or Paupack Creek, makes its way through the park, over Little Falls, pictured here, and then to Lake Wallenpaupack. (Courtesy Peter Osborne.)

For more than 10,000 years, Native Americans inhabited the region. Over thousands of years, they developed from a nomadic hunting culture to a hunting and gathering society and then to an agricultural society known as the Lenni Lenape. It is believed that the Lenapes used the Promised Land area for hunting but do not appear to have had any permanent settlements on the property that now includes the park. (Courtesy the University of the State of New York.)

Within 100 years of contact with the newly arrived European settlers, the Lenape were gone, either having moved west or assimilated into the general population. No major Native American archaeological sites have ever been uncovered on park property. (Courtesy Minisink Valley Historical Society.)

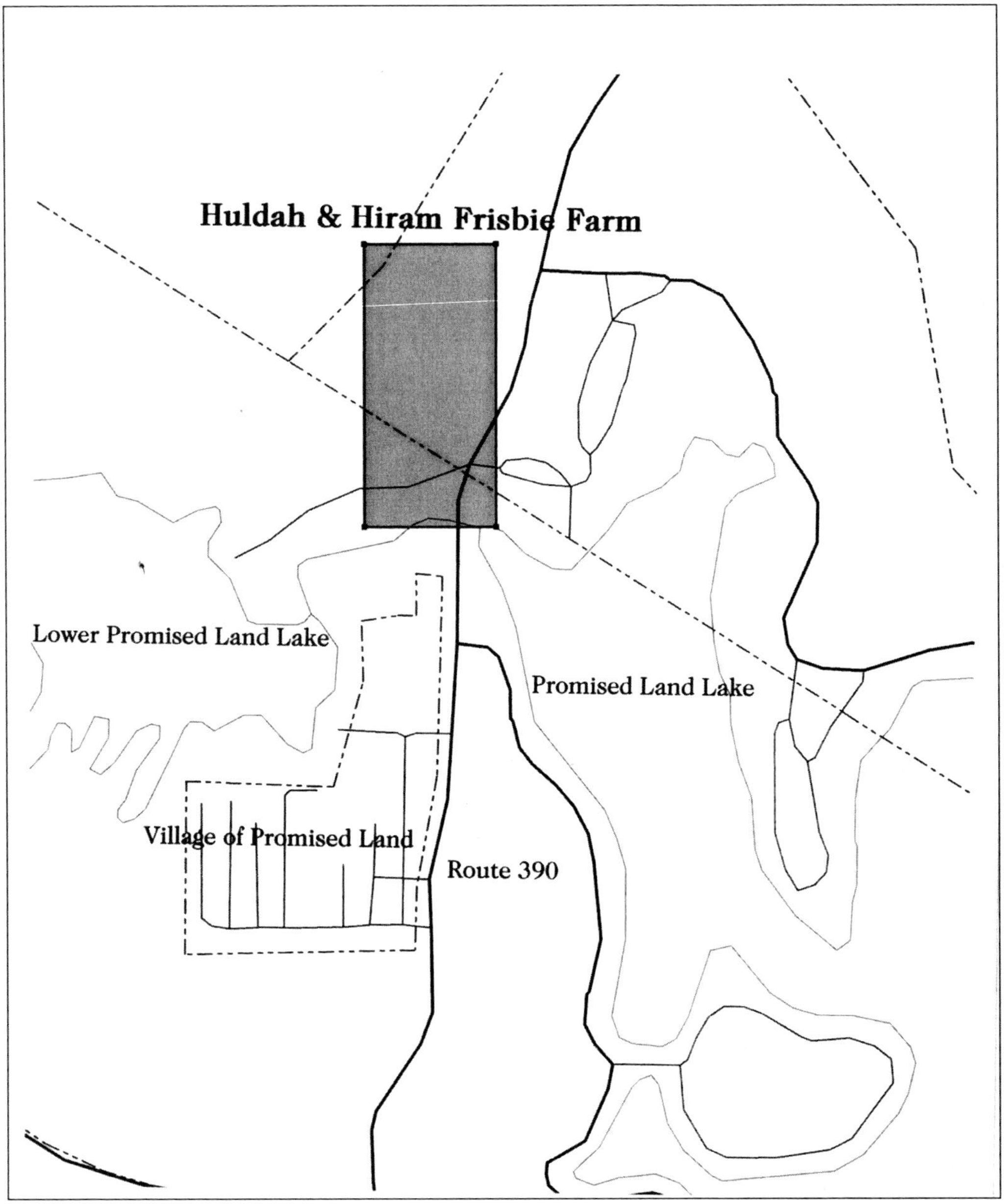

Park tradition has long held that Hiram Frisbie (1798–1882) was the first person to settle on land that now comprises the state park around 1840. However, federal census records indicate there were other settlers living in the area, so it is more accurate to say that he was among the earliest. Frisbie owned three tracts of land, one of which was within the current park boundaries. In 1834, he purchased 126 acres adjacent to the eastern boundary of the present park. In 1847, Frisbie purchased 50 acres of land adjacent to what is now Promised Land Lake, this illustration approximates its dimensions. Frisbie defaulted on the mortgage. In 1875, his wife, Huldah, purchased 98 acres in Greene township that she owned until 1888. The Frisbies lived in the area until their deaths. (Courtesy Peter Osborne and Nancy Vocci.)

After 1847, Frisbie cleared 11 acres of the land near the lake, built a house and barn, and had a cow and two oxen. He planted two apple orchards, and this tree, one of three at the main picnic area, is said to be one of the original trees or a descendant. A forester has confirmed that this tree is more than 150 years old, and it is a state park champion. (Courtesy David Heiney.)

Frow

Hiram Frisbie had at least three other businesses, including a shake mill where he was able to make shingles for roofs from bolts of wood using a frow. An 1875 map of the area near the Promised Land Lake dam also shows "Uncle Hiram's chair turning mill." Another business, a general store owned in partnership with George Simons in Greentown, only lasted a year. (Courtesy New York State Historical Association.)

Hiram Frisbie's efforts represented the early stages of what became a major theme of Pike County's history—the extraction of its natural resources. One of the most important industries in the 19th century was timbering, and two generations of lumbermen found their way to the county's forests. The first group took the prime timber and left. The second group catered to the growing mining industry. (Courtesy New York State Historical Association.)

By the 1850s, sawmills were a common sight, and lumber camps were located throughout the county. Three hundred men could clear a three-mile-square section of woodland (60,000 trees) in a season. Lumbermen were a tough lot and were accustomed to hard living. Pictured are Nathan Houck's lumber operations in nearby LaAnna. No photograph of the sawmill at Promised Land has been found. (Courtesy Greene Township Historical Society.)

Nathan Houck's woodworking factory produced umbrella sticks, clothespins, toys, flagstaffs, and during the Civil War, tent posts for the Union Army. His reserve of forestlands included a large area that encompassed Greene Township. This picture is of the Houck stick factory at LaAnna. Another lumberman, Joseph Atkinson of Hawley, began purchasing thousands of acres of forested land, which included the state park, from 1840 to 1850. (Courtesy Greene Township Historical Society.)

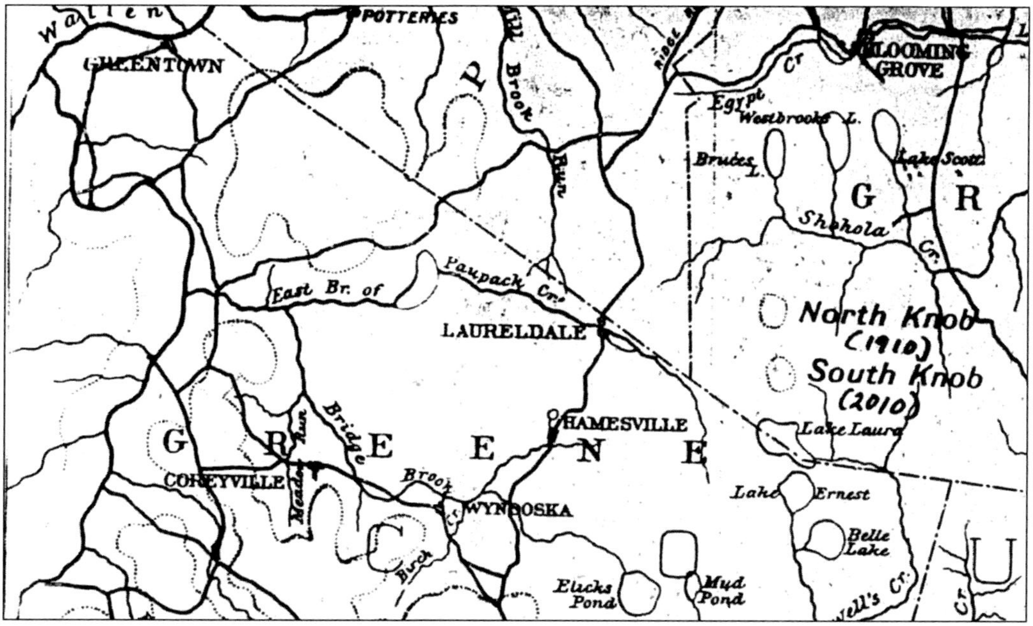

Atkinson built a crib dam using logs and boulders on the east branch of the Wallenpaupack Creek near the current dam at Promised Land Lake. From a spruce swamp, a 40-acre pond was created. Atkinson then constructed an up-and-down sawmill, one of the earliest built in Greene Township. The settlement near the dam came to be known as Laureldale; the pond is shown to the right. (Courtesy Promised Land State Park.)

The Atkinson property was sold in sections from 1850–1854 to a partnership that included two of his sons, Asher and John; Russel F. Lord (pictured here), the chief engineer of the Delaware and Hudson Canal; and T. H. R. Tracy, another canal official. The canal company's entire transportation network extended from Carbondale to Kingston, New York, more than 170 miles, and carried anthracite coal, raw materials, and finished goods. (Courtesy Minisink Valley Historical Society.)

Timber was floated to the Wallenpaupack River and then to Hawley. From there it was shipped by canal, rail, or raft to destinations all across New York and Pennsylvania. Hawley was an important stop on the Delaware and Hudson Canal, and the canal company was a transporter and consumer of timber products. Lumber was used by the company for its construction and ship building projects like this boatyard at Summitville, New York. (Courtesy Minisink Valley Historical Society.)

The canal company's Lackawaxen and Delaware aqueducts in Lackawaxen were built with timber from Promised Land. In 1870, the Promised Land tracts were sold to Dr. Joseph Jones from Honesdale. Jones built a new mill at the pond and sold bedposts, rails, and slabs. Jones's timber empire expanded around the region and into northern New York and included a short-lived business partnership with the United Society of Shakers. (Courtesy Minisink Valley Historical Society.)

The Shakers were a religious and utopian sect that settled in a number of communities in eastern New York and New England in the late 18th century and then in the West in the 19th century. The Shakers combined spiritual beliefs with work ethics to create one of the most successful sects in American history. The spiritual center of the Shakers was at New Lebanon, New York, where the first congregation was established. (Courtesy Shaker Museum and Library, Old Chatham, New York.)

In the early 1870s, the United Society of Shakers from West Pittsfield, Massachusetts, and New Lebanon, New York, consummated a partnership with Dr. Joseph Jones. In New Lebanon, they had operated a large furniture construction business along with other commercial ventures. When the partnership dissolved, the Shakers became owners of more than 10,000 acres of timberland, including the present park, forest, Bruce Lake, and Fairview Lake areas. (Courtesy Shaker Museum and Library, Old Chatham, New York.)

The Shaker community in New Lebanon, pictured here, was led by Elder Levi Shaw, at the far left. Aside from Promised Land, the Shakers had investments across the country, including lumber, flagstone, and woolen blanket businesses in Windsor, New York. When they arrived at Promised Land, the sect was in decline as membership was dropping, and their business ventures were not producing a profit. (Courtesy Shaker Museum and Library, Old Chatham, New York.)

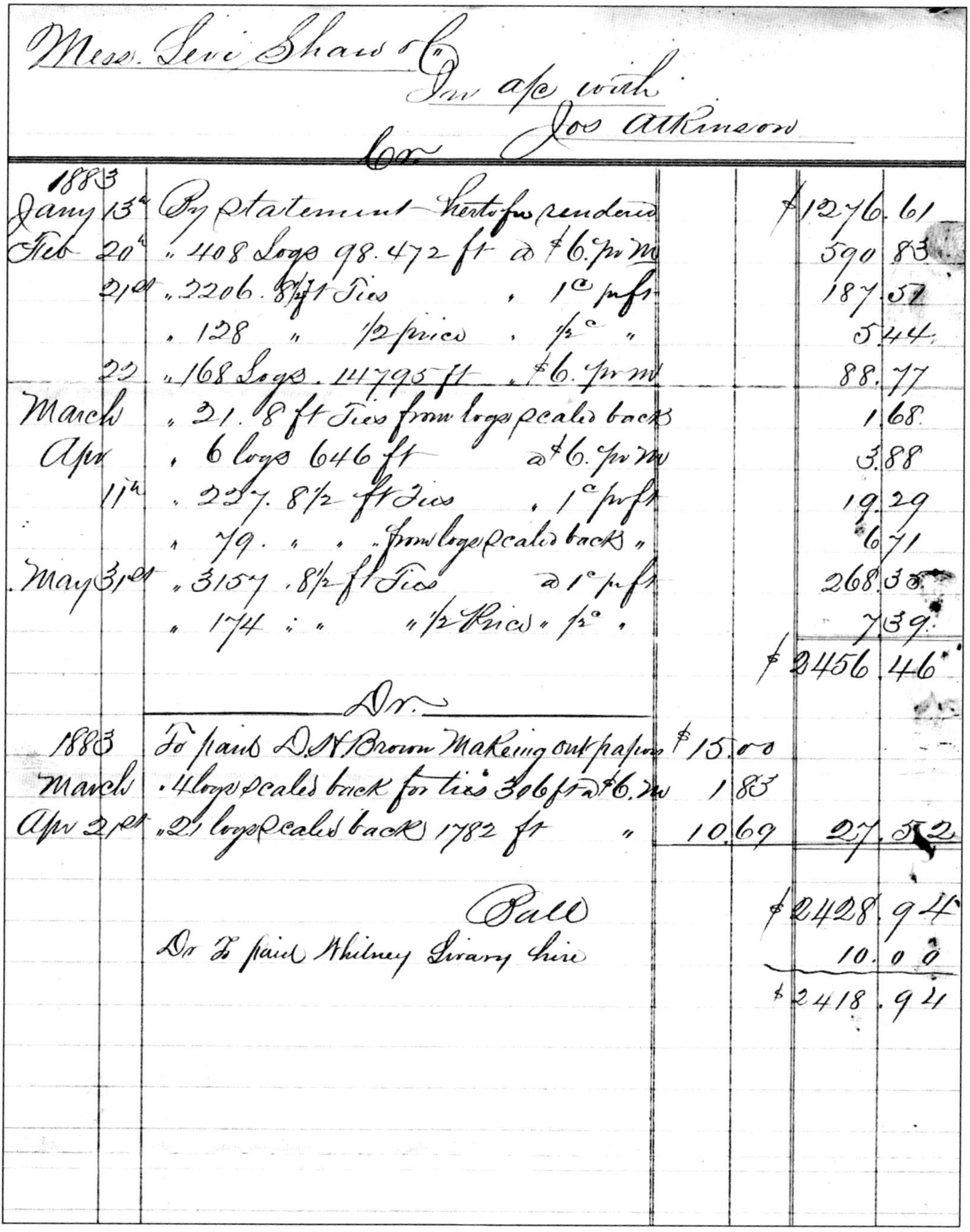

Mess. Levi Shaw & Co

In a/c with

Jos Atkinson

Cr

1883 Jany	13th	By statement heretofore rendered		$1276.61
Feb	20th	" 408 Logs 98.472 ft @ $6. pr M		590.83
	21st	" 2206. 8½ ft Ties " 1c pr ft		187.51
		" 128 " ½ price " ½c "		5.44
	22	" 168 Logs 14795 ft " $6. pr M		88.77
March		" 21. 8 ft Ties from logs scaled back		1.68
Apr		" 6 logs 646 ft @ $6. pr M		3.88
	11th	" 227. 8½ ft Ties " 1c pr ft		19.29
		" 79 " " from logs scaled back "		6.71
May	31st	" 3157 8½ ft Ties @ 1c pr ft		268.35
		" 174 " " ½ Price ½c "		7.39
				$2456.46

Dr.

1883		To paid D.N. Brown Making out papers	$15.00	
March		" 4 logs scaled back for ties 306 ft @ $6. M	1.83	
Apr	21st	" 21 logs scaled back 1782 ft "	10.69	27.52
		Ball		$2428.94
		Dr To paid Whitney Livery hire		10.00
				$2418.94

It is often thought that the Shaker investment at Promised Land was a utopian one, but it was not. It was a significant business venture intended to make money for both Shaker societies. They sold timber, mostly oak, as well as pine and hemlock bark, from their holdings, some of which might have been used back in New Lebanon. Shaw contracted with several parties to timber off the land, including Joseph Atkinson Jr. and Collingwood and Company, one of the larger sawmills in the region. The contractors used a steam-powered sawmill to cut the timber and grind bark. The contracts lasted until much of the property was cleared. (Courtesy Promised Land State Park.)

Oak, pine, chestnut, and hemlock were all timbered, and a large number of railroad ties were manufactured at Promised Land. Railroad ties like those pictured here on the Delaware and Hudson Gravity Railroad sold for 1¢ per foot if they were the highest grade. In 1899, the Shakers sold their holdings at Promised Land and Fairview Lake to William Kelly, who sold the land to Nettie Weitz in 1901. (Courtesy Minisink Valley Historical Society.)

Another important dimension of the timbering industry came about in the late 1830s, when processes were developed for the treatment of animal hides using tannic acid to make them softer before creating leather products. The region's hemlocks and oaks then became much sought after because their bark was rich in tannin. Bark was stripped from the trees in the spring and sent to the tanneries by wagon. (Courtesy Richard Gassmann.)

Hides were treated in vats containing an extract of the tannic acid made from ground oak and hemlock bark. It took about 2,000 pounds of bark to treat 200–300 pounds of leather. After being treated, the leather was used to create shoes, harnesses, and other goods and was shipped via the canal or railroad. One of the region's most important tanning operations was located in the nearby Ledgedale area. (Courtesy New York State Historical Association.)

Another important industry in the region was the harvesting of ice. Ice was cut out of local ponds in the winter, stored, and then shipped via railroad for people to use in their iceboxes. The ice was also used in the boardinghouses that serviced tourists who were vacationing in the region. People were still cutting ice for campers at Promised Land until the 1960s. (Courtesy Robert Hazelton.)

With the decline of the timber industry, the area became home to various hunting and fishing camps that were created to preserve game and fish. Adjacent to the park, the Blooming Grove Park Association, later the Blooming Grove Hunting and Fishing Club, was established and purchased thousands of acres. In nearby Fairview Lake, parcels were sold for individual cottages and later, youth camps. (Courtesy Minisink Valley Historical Society.)

The Edgar Wilson Family Genealogy

Edgar Wilson (1856-1923)
married
Mary Addie Hineline (1865-1933)

Children
Twin #1 & Twin #2 (Died at birth)
Addie Wilson (1883-c.1963) *married* William Kuntz
Jennie Wilson (1885-1972)
Charles Wilson (1886-1951)
Grant Wilson (1890-1946) *married* Clemence Olsommer
Robert Wilson (1894-1960) *married* Myrtle Hohn
Joseph Wilson (1895-1909)
Clara Wilson (1900-1901)
Martha Wilson (1904-1997) *married* Walter Keath

In the late 1800s, Edgar Wilson and his father, John, arrived in the Promised Land area and pursued timbering along with other business interests. The Wilsons were originally from Sullivan County, New York. Since their arrival in Promised Land, four generations of Wilsons have worked for or had concessions in the park, or had businesses in the nearby village, typical of many local families. (Courtesy Clayton Price, Nancy Conod, and Nancy Vocci.)

Long-time visitors will remember some of Edgar's children, including Charles Wilson, pictured overlooking Promised Land Lake at Grant Wilson's boat landing near the present-day main beach area. The Wilsons operated a boat concession until the 1960s. Robert Wilson owned a store on Route 390 that catered to locals and park visitors. Jennie Wilson was a schoolteacher and owned the Wilson Inn along with brother Charles. (Courtesy Pennsylvania State Archives.)

Edgar Wilson built the Wilson Inn, a boardinghouse, which was operated by Jennie and Charlie Wilson for many years. Among the visitors was Pennsylvania Gov. Gifford Pinchot, who later appointed Edgar to serve as the park's first ranger. As the 19th century ended, the Poconos became the center of a new recreation industry as people from the metropolitan areas began to vacation in the many hotels and boardinghouses. (Courtesy Promised Land State Park.)

As the 19th century closed, the Upper Delaware watershed, of which Promised Land is a part, became the focus of much interest. Near Wilsonville, speculators were purchasing thousands of acres to create Lake Wallenpaupack, the largest man-made lake in the commonwealth that generates electric power. Today water from Promised Land finds its way into Lake Wallenpaupack and the Delaware River. (Courtesy Minisink Valley Historical Society.)

Beginning in 1898, the commonwealth began to purchase thousands of acres of land across the state to create forest reserves to protect the watershed and to prevent the destruction of the last remaining forests. Among those first acquisitions were 439 acres that ultimately became part of Promised Land State Park. A year later, the first reforestation projects began in Pike County. (Courtesy Promised Land State Park.)

Two

A Grand Vision

As is the case with so many of our nation's most prized accomplishments, men and women, often far ahead of public opinion, have charted a course that is remarkably visionary. Such is the case with our nation's parks and forests, including those in Pennsylvania. In 1895, the state legislature created the Department of Forestry, later to become the Department of Forests and Waters. This was headed by Dr. Joseph Rothrock, the first commissioner of forestry. Soon the agency was acquiring large tracts of land across the commonwealth that came to be called the forest reserves. Initially, the department's primary concerns were reforestation, fire protection, and defense against destructive floods. The use of the property primarily as a recreational facility did not come until later. By 1907, almost 1 million acres had been acquired.

When the Department of Forestry acquired the land that now makes up Promised Land, it took control of a property that is far different from the one now seen. There were very few old growth trees left standing that had any value. The landscape was a rather desolate one—replete with stumps, eroded ground and brush, and scarce wildlife. Fires had ravaged the landscape. As one writer put it, "the land was worthless." From those early days, when the area was referred to as the Pocono Desert, has come the park that is now known and loved. Today the park is covered again with a thick forest, which supports many wildlife species.

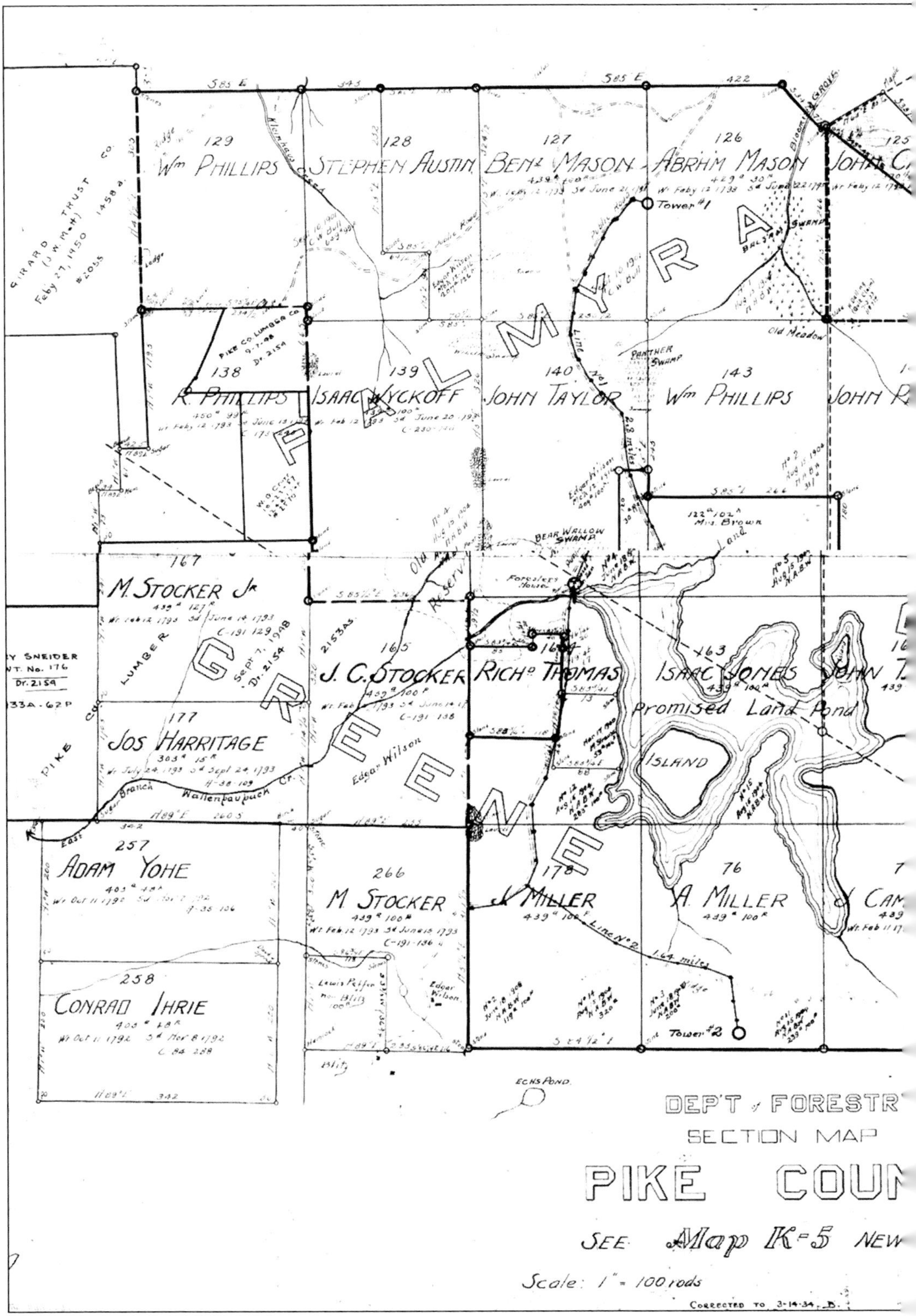
129
Wm PHILLIPS
128
STEPHEN AUSTIN
127
BENJ MASON
126
ABRHM MASON
GIRARD TRUST CO.
Tower #1
PALMYRA
PANTHER SWAMP
138
R. PHILLIPS
139
ISAAC WYCKOFF
140
JOHN TAYLOR
143
Wm PHILLIPS
BEAR WALLOW SWAMP
Foresters House
167
M. STOCKER Jr
165
J. C. STOCKER
RICHD THOMAS
163
ISAAC JONES
Promised Land Pond
ISLAND
177
JOS HARRITAGE
GREENE
Wallenpaupack Cr.
257
ADAM YOHE
266
M STOCKER
178
J MILLER
76
A. MILLER
258
CONRAD IHRIE
Tower #2
ECHS POND
DEP'T of FORESTR
SECTION MAP
PIKE COUN
SEE Map K-5 NEW
Scale: 1" = 100 rods
CORRECTED TO 3-14-34

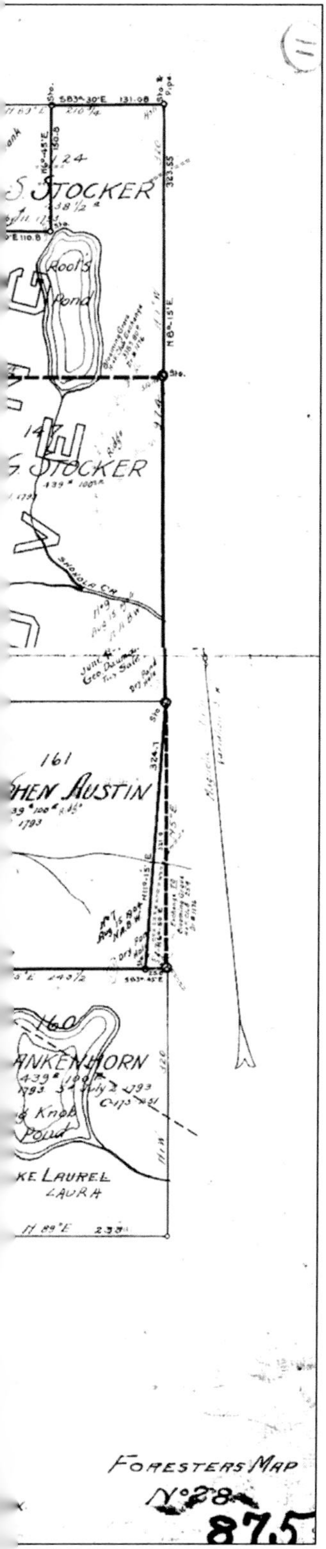

Beginning in 1898, with a tax sale purchase, the commonwealth began a 10-year effort to acquire thousands of acres that became Promised Land State Park. In 1904, the central and northern parts of the park were purchased from George and Nettie Weitz of New York City. In 1908, the last large tract that creates most of the present park and surrounding forest was also purchased from the Weitz's. In total, 6,700 acres were purchased at a price of about $2 per acre. The total cost was about $13,000. After that, the state continued to acquire additional property. This map shows the approximate borders of the park as it was configured in the 1930s. Other landowners sold land to the park, including Aaron Peck, C. W. Bull, Edgar Wilson, C. J. Rose, and Jacob Kleinhaus (Courtesy Promised Land State Park.)

Nettie Weitz was an astute businesswoman involved in real estate around the metropolitan New York City area. Her husband was a professional organist and piano craftsman. When the Weitz family purchased the Shaker land it also included several thousand acres near what is now called Fairview Lake. They built a cabin overlooking the lake and began to sell off lots around the lake. Their cabin is now a mess hall for Camp Oneka, a girl's summer camp. (Courtesy Peter Osborne.)

With the purchase of the Promised Land tracts, the state's primary concerns were reforestation and fire protection. Then the state legislature authorized funding for developing and maintaining the park. The state hired personnel, set up several primitive campgrounds, built a water supply and sanitary facilities, created a few picnic areas, and undertook forestry projects. (Courtesy Jack Cressman.)

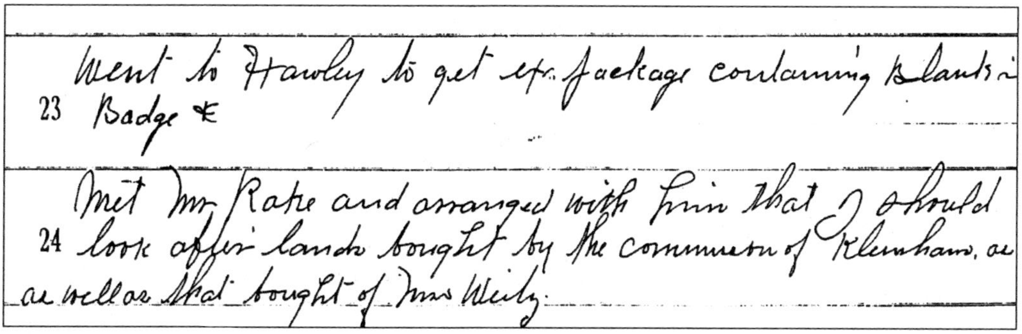

23 Went to Hawley to get exp. package containing blanks & Badge &

24 Met Mr Rake and arranged with him that I should look after lands bought by the commission of Kleinhans, as as well as that bought of Mrs Weitz.

Edgar Wilson was the first caretaker of the property; he was later appointed forest ranger, serving in this capacity until 1917. This February 1905 work report, filed by Wilson, may have been his first. In 1906, J. E. Avery, a graduate of the Pennsylvania State Forestry Academy at Mount Alto, began work as the first forester assigned to the park. (Courtesy Promised Land State Park.)

The park opened its first recreational facilities in 1905, the third state forest park to be opened for public use in which a camping area was on or near an existing lake. The first camping area was located between Bear Wallow Road and the east branch of the Wallenpaupack Creek. A nearby springhouse provided drinking water. In the early years, camping permits were not needed. (Courtesy Promised Land State Park.)

The former combination residence and office, pictured on the left, was built between 1913 and 1915. This building was one of the first constructed in a state park by the state government. Until 1990, the park's managers lived there. Located to the north of the present dam, the building was torn down in 1998 due to deterioration. An interpretive sign and stone path is all that remains. (Courtesy Promised Land State Park.)

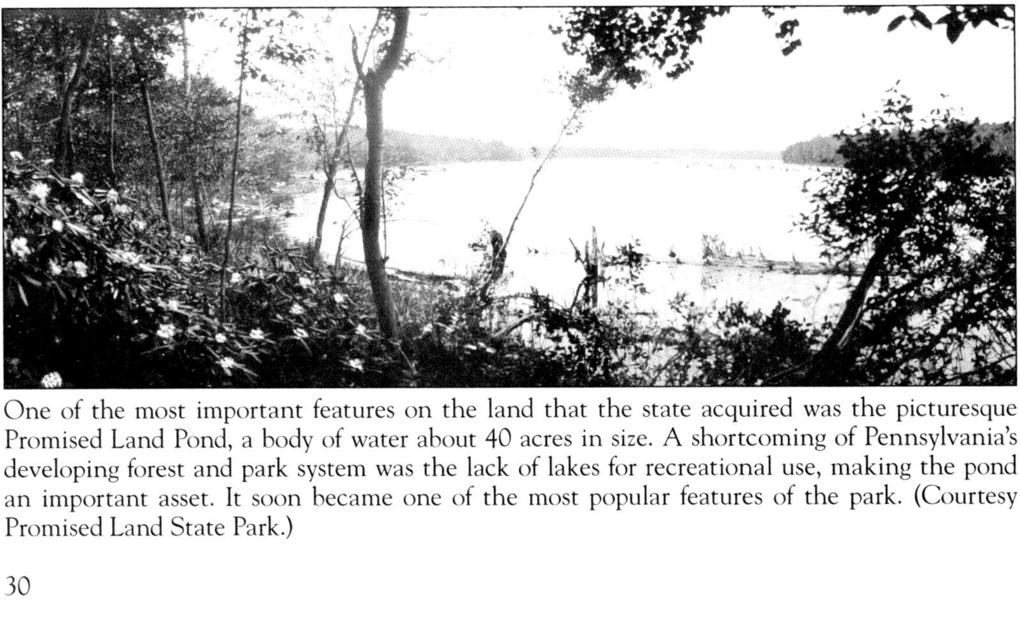

One of the most important features on the land that the state acquired was the picturesque Promised Land Pond, a body of water about 40 acres in size. A shortcoming of Pennsylvania's developing forest and park system was the lack of lakes for recreational use, making the pond an important asset. It soon became one of the most popular features of the park. (Courtesy Promised Land State Park.)

An early priority of the Department of Forestry was to enlarge Promised Land Pond. The dam that created the pond had been constructed almost 70 years before. In 1911, with an appropriation of $1,000, the earthen dam was strengthened and made taller. A much larger lake that covered about 400 acres was created. The dam is in the foreground with Route 390 behind it. (Courtesy Promised Land State Park.)

From the moment the park was opened, the focal point of park activity was located near the Promised Land Lake dam. The early picnic, boating, and camping facilities were all within a short distance of each other. Because it promoted tent camping, the park was designated a Class A public campground. The forester's house is to the left, and Route 390 is at the center. (Courtesy Promised Land State Park.)

Boats could be rented from a private concessionaire at Wilson's Landing, on the southern side of the dam. Martha Keath (née Wilson) and husband, Walter Keath, operated a grocery store, which is pictured on the left side of the photograph. The Keath store served as a restaurant, icehouse, boat-rental headquarters, and center for entertainment. (Courtesy Promised Land State Park.)

Another significant person associated with the park's long history was Henry Masker. His boat-and-bait concession lasted for more than 60 years (1920–1986). He built the first boating access to Masker's Landing, now called Ridgefield Point, and the road that leads to it from the North Shore Road. He also built 24 campsites with tables and fireplaces, all at his own expense. (Courtesy Promised Land State Park.)

In 1913, with a growing number of people coming to the park, the state established six areas for campgrounds, accommodating 35 campers each. In the same year, about 1,200 people came to the park. With the increasing numbers of visitors, it is believed that a new campground was opened in 1925 at what is now the main day-use area. The park's campgrounds along Bear Wallow Road were closed. (Courtesy Pennsylvania State Archives.)

In an effort to promote the use of state forests and parks, camping was encouraged by the offer of long-term campsite reservations. Campsites with tent platforms were constructed, as visitors stayed for extended periods and the site could be rented for the entire summer. By the end of the 1920s, recreational use of the commonwealth's parks had doubled and there were 15 state forest parks. (Courtesy Robert Koehler.)

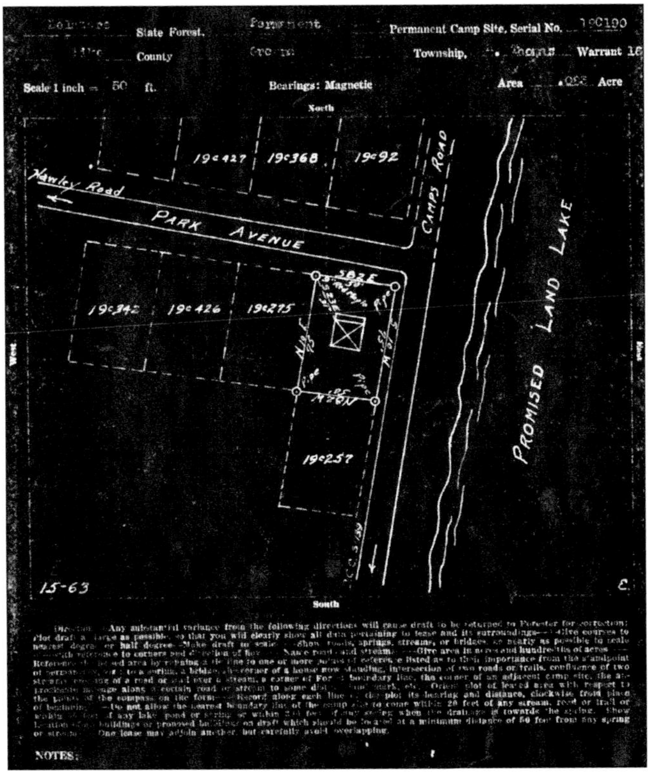

Beginning in 1913, and continuing until 1970, the state forest and park system encouraged the construction of privately owned cabins located on state land. Called leased campsites, the cabins were built by the lessee. The lease was for 10 years. Initially, there were no requirements or regulations. However, in the 1920s, the state developed approved designs on lots that were 100 feet square. (Courtesy Promised Land State Park.)

This 1921 photograph of a cabin, is a vestige of an earlier era. Two hundred and twenty five cabins were built in Promised Land; the last was constructed in 1956. Today those leased campsites are still privately owned, with 10-year leases and a set of regulatory guidelines. The Promised Land Cabin Owners Association meets regularly to discuss issues that pertain to its holdings. (Courtesy Robert Koehler.)

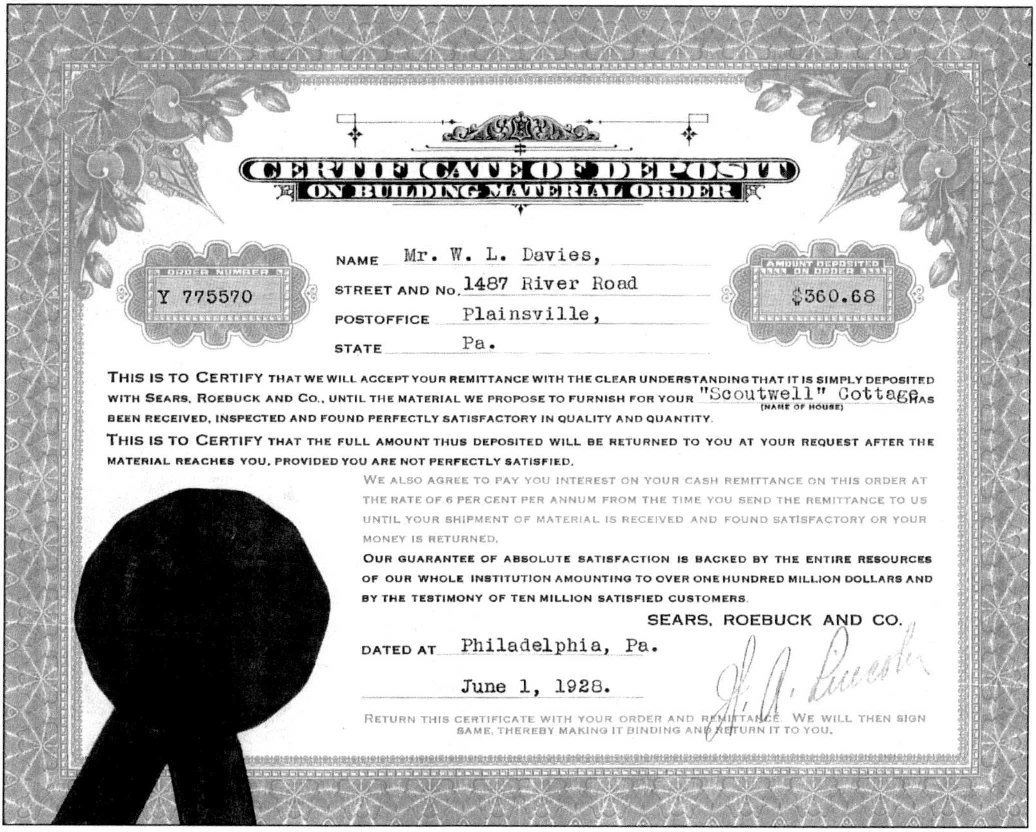

CERTIFICATE OF DEPOSIT
ON BUILDING MATERIAL ORDER

ORDER NUMBER Y 775570

NAME Mr. W. L. Davies,
STREET AND No. 1487 River Road
POSTOFFICE Plainsville,
STATE Pa.

AMOUNT DEPOSITED ON ORDER $360.68

THIS IS TO CERTIFY THAT WE WILL ACCEPT YOUR REMITTANCE WITH THE CLEAR UNDERSTANDING THAT IT IS SIMPLY DEPOSITED WITH SEARS, ROEBUCK AND CO., UNTIL THE MATERIAL WE PROPOSE TO FURNISH FOR YOUR "Scoutwell" Cottage (NAME OF HOUSE) HAS BEEN RECEIVED, INSPECTED AND FOUND PERFECTLY SATISFACTORY IN QUALITY AND QUANTITY.

THIS IS TO CERTIFY THAT THE FULL AMOUNT THUS DEPOSITED WILL BE RETURNED TO YOU AT YOUR REQUEST AFTER THE MATERIAL REACHES YOU, PROVIDED YOU ARE NOT PERFECTLY SATISFIED.

WE ALSO AGREE TO PAY YOU INTEREST ON YOUR CASH REMITTANCE ON THIS ORDER AT THE RATE OF 6 PER CENT PER ANNUM FROM THE TIME YOU SEND THE REMITTANCE TO US UNTIL YOUR SHIPMENT OF MATERIAL IS RECEIVED AND FOUND SATISFACTORY OR YOUR MONEY IS RETURNED.

OUR GUARANTEE OF ABSOLUTE SATISFACTION IS BACKED BY THE ENTIRE RESOURCES OF OUR WHOLE INSTITUTION AMOUNTING TO OVER ONE HUNDRED MILLION DOLLARS AND BY THE TESTIMONY OF TEN MILLION SATISFIED CUSTOMERS.

SEARS, ROEBUCK AND CO.

DATED AT Philadelphia, Pa.
June 1, 1928.

RETURN THIS CERTIFICATE WITH YOUR ORDER AND REMITTANCE. WE WILL THEN SIGN SAME, THEREBY MAKING IT BINDING AND RETURN IT TO YOU.

The numbering system used for each cabin indicates that it is in the 19th forest district, that it is a cabin, and the chronological order in which it was assigned. At least one of the cabins in Promised Land (19-C-460) was constructed in 1928 using a building package from Sears and Roebuck. This certificate from Sears came with the building materials. (Courtesy William Davies.)

Early on, the Department of Forestry began to reclaim the land by managing the remaining timber resources and undertaking extensive reforestation. Between 1911 and 1919, thousands of white pine, Norway spruce, red oak, elm, sugar maple, and willow seedlings were planted. Some of the pines are shown here in 1924. During this time, diseases struck many trees in the park, causing considerable damage. (Courtesy Promised Land State Park.)

The park was home to several forestry demonstration projects. Willow cuttings were planted to provide materials for prison inmates to create baskets. To grow trees in the hardpan ground, areas of the park were dynamited to see if it would loosen the hardpan, allowing for better growth. It did not. Today trees planted more than 75 years ago still stand in their plantations, like these white pines near the day-use area. (Courtesy Peter Osborne.)

Another task for the Department of Forestry was fire suppression and protection. One forest fire claimed 200 acres of the park and 250 acres of adjoining private land in 1913. As a result, two forest fire towers were constructed, called the North and South Fire Towers. They were used until the late 1930s, when the forest had recovered to such a degree that there was only limited visibility from them. (Courtesy Robert Koehler.)

When the commonwealth assumed ownership of the property, there were old lumber roads that crisscrossed it. Present-day Route 390 divided the park and was the main access road from both the north and south. Then a dirt road, it was difficult to travel when muddy and could be impassible in the winter. (Courtesy Robert Koehler.)

With the growing demand on the park's resources, a right-of-way and service road was built from North Shore Road to Ridgefield Point in 1922 by Henry Masker to service his boat concession. It was not until the mid-1930s that the road around the lake was completed. Park Avenue, pictured here, was also built, running along the western shore of Promised Land Lake. (Courtesy Jack Cressman.)

One of the most architecturally significant structures in the park, Whittaker Lodge was built by the state before 1930. This log cabin is located on a peninsula at the northeastern end of Promised Land Lake. Typical of the lodges of the time, it has always been used for forestry department personnel and agency activities. It was named for Thomas Whittaker, the forest ranger at the park from 1924 to 1936. (Courtesy Promised Land State Park.)

From the very beginning, camping has been a popular activity at Promised Land. As automobiles became available to the growing middle class in the early 1900s, travel trailers were developed to bring camping equipment to the park for vacations. As a result of the growing number of parks and the popularity of them, a Bureau of Parks was created in 1929. (Courtesy Harry Leitheiser.)

Three

We Can Take It! The Arrival of the Civilian Conservation Corps

It is against this backdrop of America on the move, enjoying its new national and state parks and forests, that the Great Depression descended upon the nation and lasted from 1929 to 1941. Thousands of banks collapsed, the stock market dropped precipitously, and the nation witnessed unprecedented poverty and unemployment. The nation's land had been devastated by years of poor management practices in its forests and farms. Huge clouds of dust, which later caused the decade to become known as the "dirty thirties," rolled east from the Midwest and Great Plains.

In 1932, New York governor Franklin D. Roosevelt defeated Pres. Herbert Hoover. Roosevelt called for a New Deal for the American people. In March 1933, he had his cabinet draw up plans to put young men to work in the parks and forests of the country. By June 1933, the Civilian Conservation Corps (CCC) had been created by an act entitled "Emergency Conservation Work." For the first time in American history, four different cabinet agencies, the departments of Labor, Interior, War, and Agriculture, all worked together to manage the affairs of the CCC with its director, Robert Fechner, who coordinated the program.

The CCC's eight years in Promised Land were transformative, especially when one places their work in the context of what had happened in the previous decades. Prior to the CCC, there was little funding available to develop all of the resources at the park. For Pennsylvania, the CCC would provide the greatest state park development program of all time.

Gov. Gifford Pinchot (1865–1946), the first chief of the U.S. Forest Service, was a member of President Roosevelt's brain trust when it came to the creation of the CCC. Prior to the creation of the CCC, Governor Pinchot had men who were on relief working in camps in parks and forests across Pennsylvania. Pennsylvania had the second highest number of CCC camps in the country. (Courtesy Minisink Valley Historical Society.)

President Roosevelt's plan was to assist the hundreds of thousands of young men who were unemployed through no fault of their own. It is estimated that one quarter of the men ages 18 to 25 were unemployed during the Depression. However, the Depression affected all young men whether they were from farms, cities, or small towns. They became the cardinal concern of the CCC. (Reprinted from *We Can Take It: A Short Story of the* CCC.)

The administration of the camp at Promised Land, along with thousands of other CCC camps, was a collaborative effort between the federal departments of Labor, War (United States Army), Interior, and, in the case of state or national forests, the Department of Agriculture through the U.S. Forest Service. The state's Department of Forest and Waters coordinated the work program locally. Here, the entire administration poses in front of the bluestone sign that greeted visitors in the early 1930s. The U.S. Army ran the camp, overseeing sanitation, food, maintenance, discipline, payroll, and its own transportation needs. Throughout the years, the turnover of the military was fairly regular. The army tried to expose as many of its officers to the management of camps as possible. The army believed it was helpful to its officer corps. (Courtesy Promised Land State Park.)

Many former CCC boys describe life in camp as being similar to the military. However, they were not required to salute officers nor did they receive any military training. While camps were run by army officers until the last year of their operation, the enrollees also had much more freedom than soldiers. Pictured are two of the military commanders stationed at Promised Land. (Courtesy Promised Land State Park.)

Dewey Streepy served as the first work project superintendent and represented the state's Department of Forests and Waters. He provided oversight of the work projects on behalf of the state and was responsible for the men's activities during the day. He also kept the camp's paperwork. He served from 1933 to 1938 and was succeeded by Van Brion and then Garland Inscoe. Project superintendents were paid $225 per month. (Courtesy Promised Land State Park.)

Tom Frantz, one of the foremen on the staff, oversaw the forestry projects. Foremen received between $150 to $170 per month and came from all walks of life. Some were college graduates, others were master craftsmen, and some had risen up through the ranks of the CCC boys. Most of the time there were six or seven foremen on duty overseeing work projects. (Courtesy Promised Land State Park.)

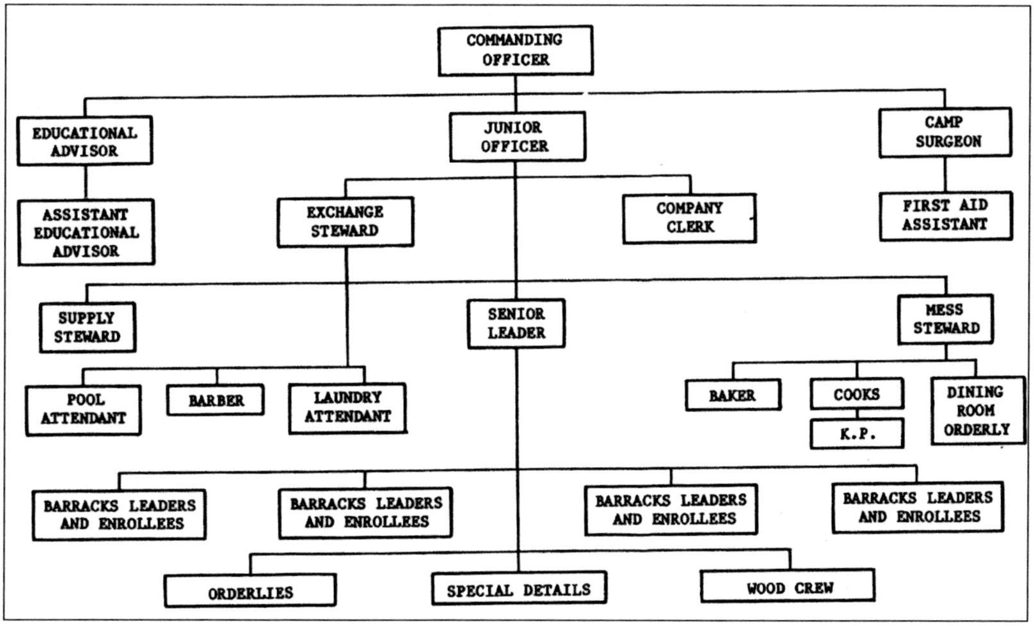

Each CCC company had 200 men, known as enrollees, although that number was not always maintained. There were four kinds of companies—junior enrollees, World War I veterans, African American, and Native American. Native Americans worked on their own reservations; African Americans worked in segregated camps. Pictured here is the organizational chart for a typical CCC company as each man was ranked and leadership was developed from within the ranks. (Courtesy National Archives Records Administration, 35-12, 9.)

To signify their ranks or positions, CCC boys wore patches on their uniforms. Pictured here is a hat with the general organizational patch and patches representing some of the various positions including baker, cook, librarian, and quartermaster. Another layer of leadership came from the so-called "LEMs", the local experienced men, who were knowledgeable at working outdoors and could help the enrollees adapt to their new situation. (Courtesy Promised Land State Park.)

Three companies passed through Promised Land, including Company 337 (May 1933–May 1936), pictured here. These men came mainly from the Philadelphia area. Company 5463 (May 1936–October 1937) was organized in Fort McClelland, Alabama. The third company, 1399 (October 1937–July 1941), was in the camp until its closure. Originally made up of World War I veterans, the company was organized at Fort George Meade, Maryland, and came from the Dingmans Ferry, Pennsylvania, area after the CCC camp located near there was closed. (Courtesy Promised Land State Park.)

Company 337 was initially organized at Fort Hoyle, Maryland, on May 5, 1933, and arrived the next day at the Delaware, Lackawanna, and Western's railroad station in Cresco, Pennsylvania, south of the park. Cresco was the camp's nearest station. In later years, Gouldsboro was used as the camp's official railroad station. Today the Cresco Station Museum is home to the Barrett Township Historical Society. (Courtesy Peter Osborne.)

When the first CCC boys arrived at Promised Land, they stayed in tents near the present picnic ground, moving into their permanent winter quarters near the entrance of Pickerel Point later that fall. The camp was one of the first created in the state; its motto was "It Shall be Done." (Courtesy Promised Land State Park.)

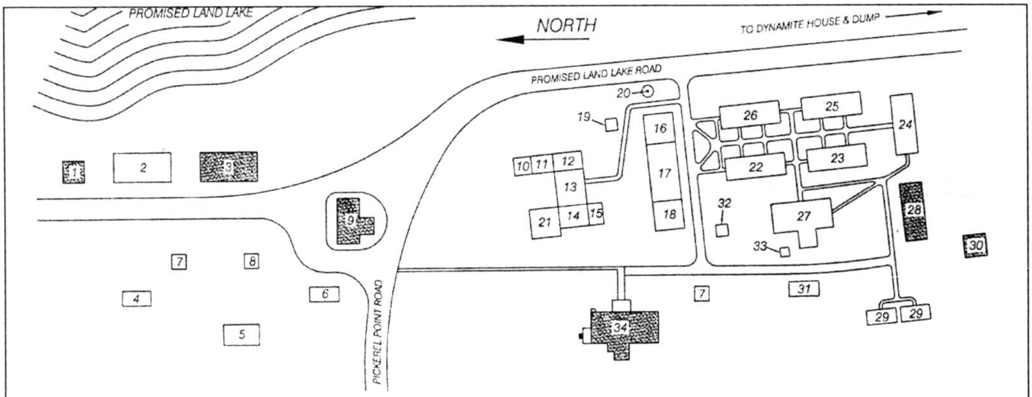

NUMBER	DESCRIPTIONS	NUMBER	DESCRIPTIONS
1	BLACKSMITH SHOP	18	SICK BAY
2	STORAGE GARAGE	19	FEDERAL MEDICAL HEADQUARTERS
3	STORAGE SUPPLY (PRESENT DAY GARAGE)	20	FLAGPOLE
4	GARAGE	21	SHOP
5	REPAIR SHOP	22	BARRACKS #1
6	TOOL SHED	23	BARRACKS #2
7	GENERATOR	24	BARRACKS #3
8	OIL & GAS HOUSE	25	BARRACKS #4
9	CAMP SUPERINTENDENT'S OFFICE & STATE TECH. SERVICES (PRESENT DAY EEO)	26	BARRACKS #5 - TOP-KICK'S QUARTERS, CLOTHING SUPPLIES, & COMPANY STAFF
10	CHAPEL	27	MESS HALL
11	STAGE	28	WASH HOUSE & BARBER SHOP (PRESENT DAY AUDITORIUM)
12	WOODWORKING SHOP	29	LATRINES
13	DANCE FLOOR	30	PUMP HOUSE
14	POOL TABLE & PING-PONG TABLE	31	SPUD HOUSE & COOK SUPPLIES
15	CANTEEN	32	ARMY MEDICAL HEADQUARTERS
16	MEDICAL OFFICE	33	GREASE PIT
17	OFFICERS' QUARTERS	34	FOREMAN'S QUARTERS (PRESENT DAY MUSEUM)

This drawing illustrates what the permanent camp looked like at the peak of its activity in 1938, with 24 buildings. Each CCC camp was concentrated in one location, and it was estimated that a typical camp spent $5,000 per month to operate. When all of the administrative costs were included, it cost about $180,000 per year to operate a CCC camp. (Courtesy Kenneth Naugle.)

Camps were designated with a special numbering system. The CCC camp at Promised Land was known for most of its existence as Camp S-139. "S" designated state forest and the camp number coincided with the Army Corps district, as did the company numbers. A large sign welcoming visitors stood at the entrance to the permanent camp near Pickerel Point. In later years, it was known as Camp Pocono. (Courtesy Promised Land State Park.)

This view of the camp is looking south, with barracks buildings on both sides. Army officers and Department of Forestry supervisors who were single, or whose families were elsewhere, lived full-time at the camp. Some lived in nearby towns and commuted home on weekends. Enrollees maintained the buildings and improved their appearance by creating walkways and chestnut guardrails, painting white stone borders, and planting trees. (Courtesy Promised Land State Park.)

Enrollees lived in a simple barracks building that housed 40 men and measured 20 feet by 112 feet. Room and board were considered part of their compensation. The barracks were heated by coal stoves, one of which is pictured on the right. Medical care was available at all times and was provided at no charge; a doctor was on call. An on-site infirmary handled minor medical problems. Fatal injuries in the CCC were uncommon. (Courtesy Promised Land State Park.)

Each man was assigned a bed and a footlocker, or sometimes a closet. Footlockers were given personal touches, including previous CCC experience and girlfriends' names. Personal appearance, cleanliness, and physical well-being were important hallmarks of the CCC. CCC boys were given toilet kits and had to do their own wash. Each company had at least one member who could cut hair for a nickel. (Courtesy Peter Osborne.)

Hearty and healthy food was served at CCC camps. On average, an enrollee gained between 10 and 15 pounds because many had come from impoverished homes. Food was bought locally to support the local economy and farmers. Pictured is the interior of the mess hall; breakfast and dinner were served here. A bulletin board told enrollees who had kitchen police duty or fire watch and other camp news. (Courtesy Promised Land State Park.)

The cooking staff at Promised Land stands ready to serve up quality meals for hungry enrollees. Many CCC boys learned good eating habits that remained with them long after their enrollment. Many CCC cooks went on to professional careers in the food business after their enrollments were complete. (Courtesy Promised Land State Park.)

Usually lunch was served at the job site and boys ate their lunch outdoors. If the weather was cold, a hot meal was served. Typically a lunch consisted of a sandwich, fruit, and something to drink. Enterprising lads would start a fire to toast their bread or warm their meals. (Courtesy Promised Land State Park.)

WAR
FINANCE

BROOKLYN, N. Y., June 12 1936

391, 578

3 Treasurer of the United States 15-51

PAY TO THE ORDER OF Francis Bowerman --
34 Forester St. Rochester N Y

$1.00

THE SUM OF One & no/100 --

DOLLARS

OBJECT FOR WHICH DRAWN

M. T. LEGG
FINANCE OFFICER, U. S. A.

E. C. W. Vo. No. 4268

BY

229-378

CCC boys were paid $30 per month, of which $25 was sent home to family members or guardians. The boys received $2.50 every other week. The CCC provided room and board, health care, clothing, two weeks vacation, and several holidays. A CCC boy kept this uncashed CCC check as a token. When an enrollee's time was done, he was given transportation back to his hometown. (Courtesy family of Francis Leo Bowerman.)

When new enrollees like these came into a CCC camp, they were known as rookies. Enrollees were required to take orientation courses at the beginning of their enlistments. Rookies were often subject to pranks. They were sent to guard the flagpole, get skyhooks, or sent to Promised Land Lake to "reel in the shoreline." But soon enough they too were playing pranks on newcomers. (Courtesy Promised Land State Park.)

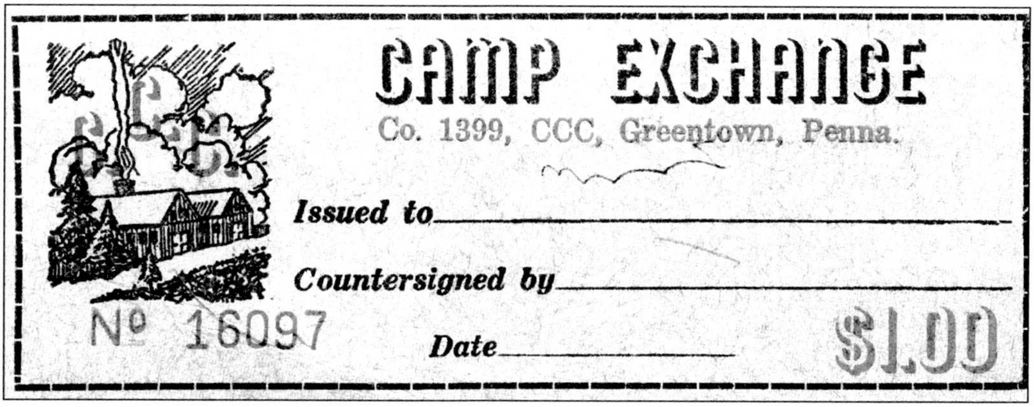
CAMP EXCHANGE

Co. 1399, CCC, Greentown, Penna.

Issued to____________________

Countersigned by____________________

No 16097 Date__________ $1.00

The PX, or canteen, at Camp Pocono was where enrollees bought candy, cigarettes, and necessities. They could also buy postcards, scrapbooks, and film using camp exchange tickets like the one pictured. Film was sent to developers across the country, processed, and then returned to the enrollee. Profits were used to benefit the camp's recreation programs. (Courtesy Promised Land State Park.)

Some CCC camps had their own distinctive items sold in the canteen. Match covers were emblazoned with the camp name and company number and are now collector's items. Pre-printed albums were sold, and a CCC boy could keep track of his best and worst moments as well as display photographs, autographs, and work records. (Courtesy Promised Land State Park.)

For camp news, enrollees turned to an in-house newsletter. With each company came a different masthead. The *Promised Land-er* was the product of the work of Company 5463. In earlier years, the camp's newsletter was called the *Timberline* (1933–1936). Newsletters also provided moral guidance, practical work advice, and information on current events and camp happenings. Copies were 10¢ for enrollees, and an additional 5¢ for those that were mailed somewhere. (Courtesy The Center for Research Libraries Collection.)

The CCC provided educational classes for the enrollees at Promised Land. The program came to be known as "the School of the Woods" and included job training and access to a camp library and traveling libraries. Twenty-six classes in reading, writing, business mathematics, English, spelling, geography, forestry, and arithmetic were offered. Teachers from the Works Progress Administration (WPA) in Scranton also taught at the camp. (Courtesy Promised Land State Park.)

CIVILIAN CONSERVATION CORPS

U.C. 978927

Unit Certificate

THIS CERTIFIES THAT ______________________ of Company ________ has satisfactorily completed ________ hours of instruction in ______________________ and is therefore granted this Certificate.

Project Superintendent.

Company Commander.

Camp Educational Adviser.

Date ________ Place ________

GPO 6—9671

CCC boys obtained important life skills during their enrollments; for example, a motor vehicle operator's permit was a valuable item to obtain. Not only did it keep the boys from some of the more unpleasant chores in camp like KP (kitchen police), it was a valuable asset when they left the CCC and went back into the private sector. Many went on to become truck drivers. Pictured is Cornelius McHugh's certificate for driving a truck. (Courtesy Promised Land State Park.)

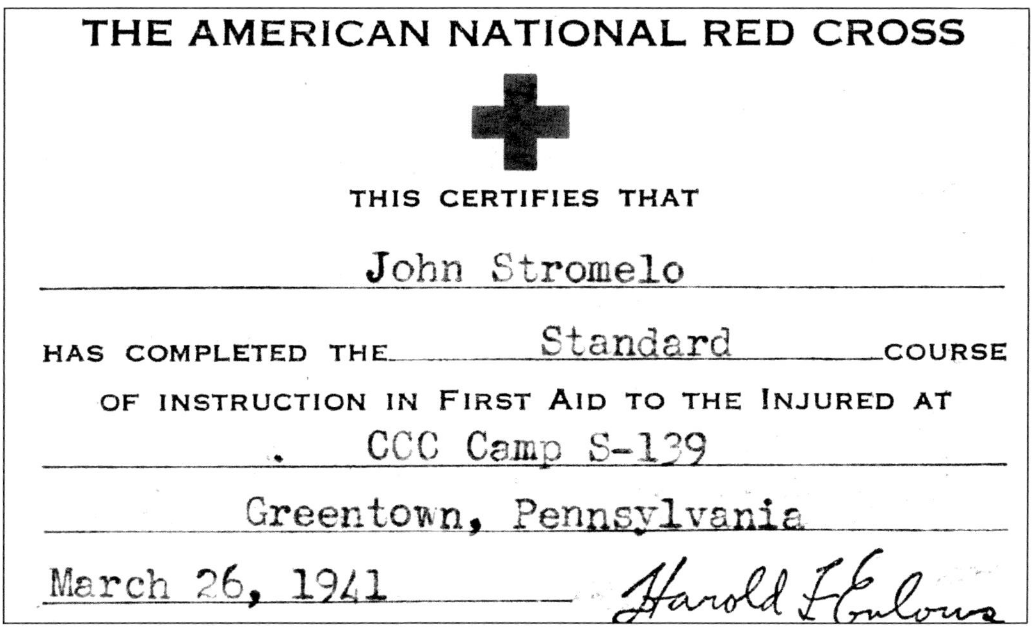

THE AMERICAN NATIONAL RED CROSS

THIS CERTIFIES THAT

John Stromelo

HAS COMPLETED THE Standard COURSE

OF INSTRUCTION IN FIRST AID TO THE INJURED AT

CCC Camp S-139

Greentown, Pennsylvania

March 26, 1941

Other courses included first aid, given by the American National Red Cross. John Stromelo, an enrollee at Promised Land, attended the standard first aid course while in the CCC and received this certification. Since 45 percent of the men had never been employed and only 13 percent had graduated from high school, the various education programs were an important component of the CCC. (Courtesy Promised Land State Park.)

After their workday was completed, CCC boys were free to do what they pleased. Boys were brought into town in the army's trucks, and the boys shopped in local stores, ate in restaurants, and went to the movies in nearby Hawley, Newfoundland, Greentown, and Scranton. Enrollees drank 5¢ beers in local bars if they were of age or if the bartenders were willing to serve them. (Courtesy Jack Cressman.)

On their days off, enrollees went swimming at the public beach at Promised Land Lake and took advantage of the attractions in the park and in the surrounding area. Responsible CCC boys could take a lifesaving course and then serve as lifeguards at public facilities, including those frequented by the CCC enrollees. (Courtesy Promised Land State Park.)

Sports, especially boxing, were popular in CCC camps across the country. Most CCC camps, including the one at Camp Pocono, had a boxing team. Other sports included baseball, basketball, skating, ping-pong, handball, swimming, canoeing, fishing, and pool. Skiing was very popular in the 1930s, as well as other winter sports, including ice-skating. The company at Promised Land even had its own ice hockey team. (Courtesy Promised Land State Park.)

The camp's administration encouraged boys to put on shows to display their talents. Enrollees attended dances in the recreation hall, where campers were invited to mingle with them. For one dance, in June 1935, 150 people turned out. There was even a camp orchestra created by Company 1399 called the Pocono Polka Dots. Listening to the radio was another popular activity. (Courtesy Promised Land State Park.)

The young men often had pictures of women in their lockers and trunks, and this cartoon reflects the thoughts of many CCC boys who were hoping to find a future mate. Most had never been away from home for extended periods of time prior to their service in the CCC. Some parents forbade their daughters to date CCC boys. Inevitably, the interaction between the CCC boys and local girls occasionally resulted in a "CCC marriage." (Courtesy Promised Land State Park.)

Photography was a popular hobby in CCC camps across the country. With the introduction of inexpensive cameras and developing services, many enrollees took photographs that now form the basis for what is known about camp life. There were even photography classes sponsored by the camp. (Courtesy Promised Land State Park.)

Occasionally CCC boys displayed their sense of humor and mischievousness in photographs as they are here, posing with the cement mixer. However, safety was an overriding concern in the CCC. Proper equipment was distributed, and safety instruction lessons by the army and Department of Forests and Waters were regularly given. Only one CCC boy was killed at Promised Land—in a truck accident in Gouldsboro. (Courtesy Promised Land State Park.)

The few enrollees who shirked their duties were known as "goldbrickers." As a penalty, they were assigned some of the more unpleasant tasks in camp. If a boy left the CCC without permission it was said that he had "gone over the hill." If he served his full term and performed his duties satisfactorily he was given an honorable discharge. (Reprinted from *We Can Take It: A Short Story of the CCC*.)

Homesickness was a major problem in the CCC, and enrollees were encouraged to write home often. Another problem was the enrollees known as "the wise guys," men who left their barracks dirty or did not do as they were told. For them, KP (kitchen police) duty was common. Enrollees were not allowed to have cars or motorcycles. (Reprinted from *We Can Take It: A Short Story of the* CCC.)

At the end of their service, CCC boys were given discharges and were released from service. At Camp Pocono, there were parties to send the men off to their new lives. An average enrollee spent nine months in the CCC, but some spent as long as the maximum allowed, two years. Enrollees who were experienced and rated, or ranked, sometimes stayed longer. (Courtesy Promised Land State Park.)

Four

The Civilian Conservation Corps Work Projects at Promised Land State Park

When the CCC arrived at Promised Land State Park, most of the park's acreage was not accessible to the public because it lacked good roads and facilities. The park still reflected the land use practices of the previous timbering generation and the early efforts of the Department of Forests and Waters. One of the first priorities of the state officials under the CCC was to build new roads and truck trails and to improve old logging roads.

Another task was to improve the forest stand. Thousands of trees were planted, numerous fire suppression projects undertaken, wildlife improvement projects constructed, and streams improved. Finally, new camping and picnicking facilities were created, along with hiking trails, cabins, parking areas, beaches, and a lake. These efforts allowed the use of a larger percentage of the property and eliminated some of the heavy congestion in the picnic area. The CCC also worked on projects outside the park in Forest District 19.

By 1941, when the camp closed, the park had been transformed into the modern multi-use park it is today. So strong is the influence of the work of the CCC boys that Promised Land is still called a CCC park, and the history of the CCC remains a primary emphasis of the park's educational efforts. Nationally, it was thought that forest conservation efforts had been advanced by 40 years because of the CCC. The work of the CCC was also the basis for the next round of improvements at the park that were undertaken after World War II.

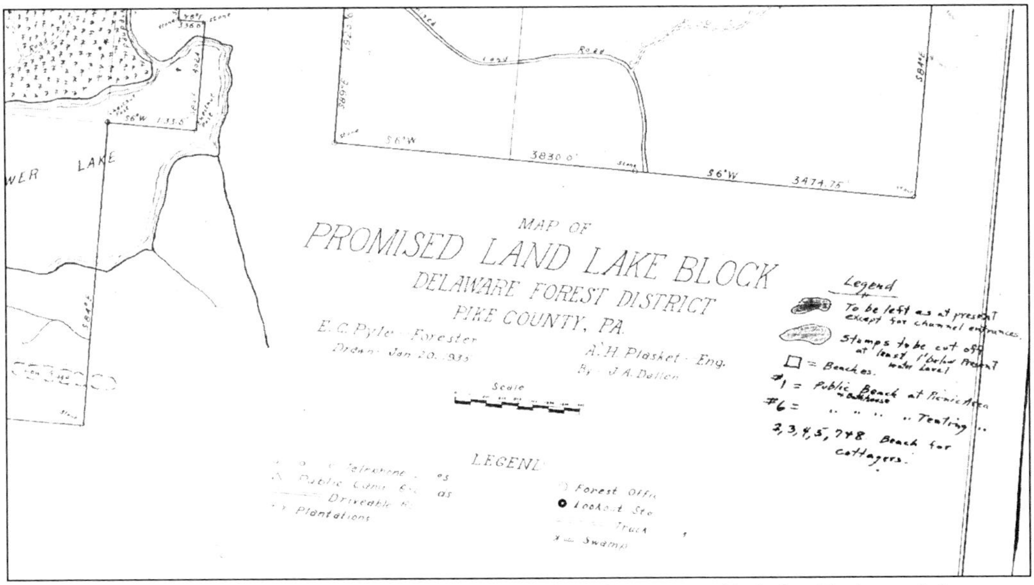

Upon arriving in Greentown, designers, working for what was called the Technical Services, created an inventory of what was already in the park, as well as a base map with elevations and boundaries. As in all CCC projects, parks were developed to give them a consistent appearance across the country. (Courtesy Promised Land State Park.)

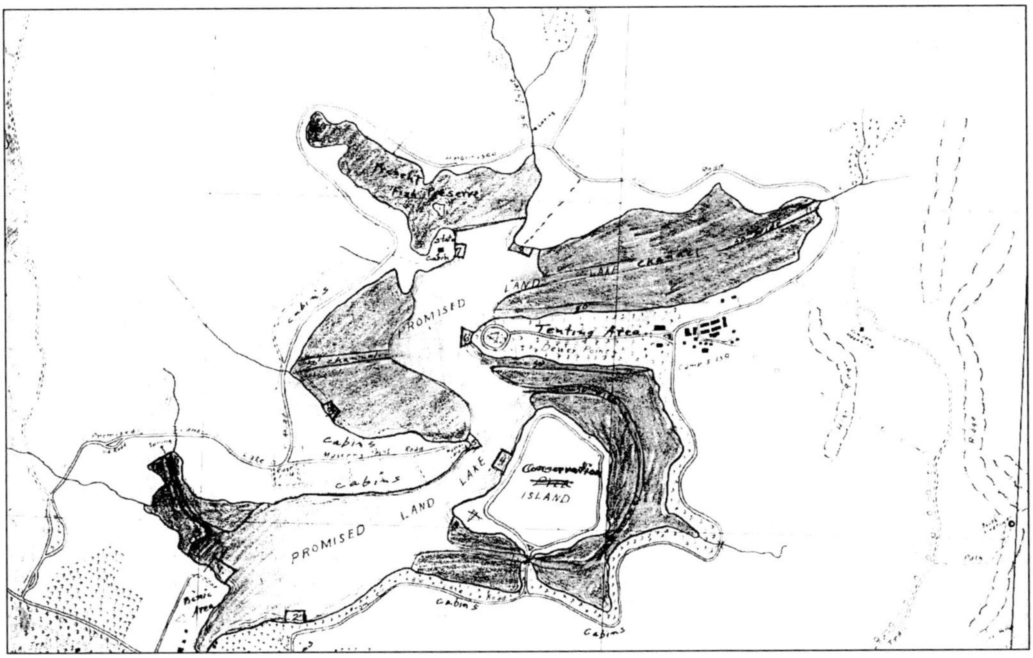

Once the base maps were completed, designers began to create a master plan. The master plan included roads, utilities, lakes, streams, and proposed construction projects. Work progress plans like this one for clearing stumps in the lake were typical. Each work period, reports were prepared for regional and national offices to show what work had been accomplished and to show what was planned. (Courtesy Promised Land State Park.)

Shop drawings for the foremen were then created for use in the field by the engineers. CCC boys who showed an aptitude for design were often trained to read the drawings and in some cases turned their experience into careers. (Courtesy Promised Land State Park.)

The CCC provided heavy equipment necessary to undertake the major projects like the building of the roads. On average, the army had three trucks, and the CCC had 15 trucks in camp. One of camp's enrollees, John Sims, received an award for being the best CCC truck driver in the state. (Courtesy Promised Land State Park.)

After the initial organization of the CCC, the state was able to acquire heavy equipment for the various camps that the CCC boys were trained to use. Here, a bulldozer operated by an enrollee brings in logs for building the Bear Wallow cabins. Camp Pocono had its own gasoline pump and oil supply, which was located near the garages. There was also a repair and blacksmith shop for equipment and tools. (Courtesy Promised Land State Park.)

Enrollees gathered in front of the technical services garages every morning at 8:00 a.m. to receive their work assignments and to be transported to job sites where they worked until 4:00 p.m. The men rode in open-stake body trucks that were covered with canvas tarps during the winter or severe weather. A considerable number of workdays were lost to inclement weather in Promised Land. (Courtesy Promised Land State Park.)

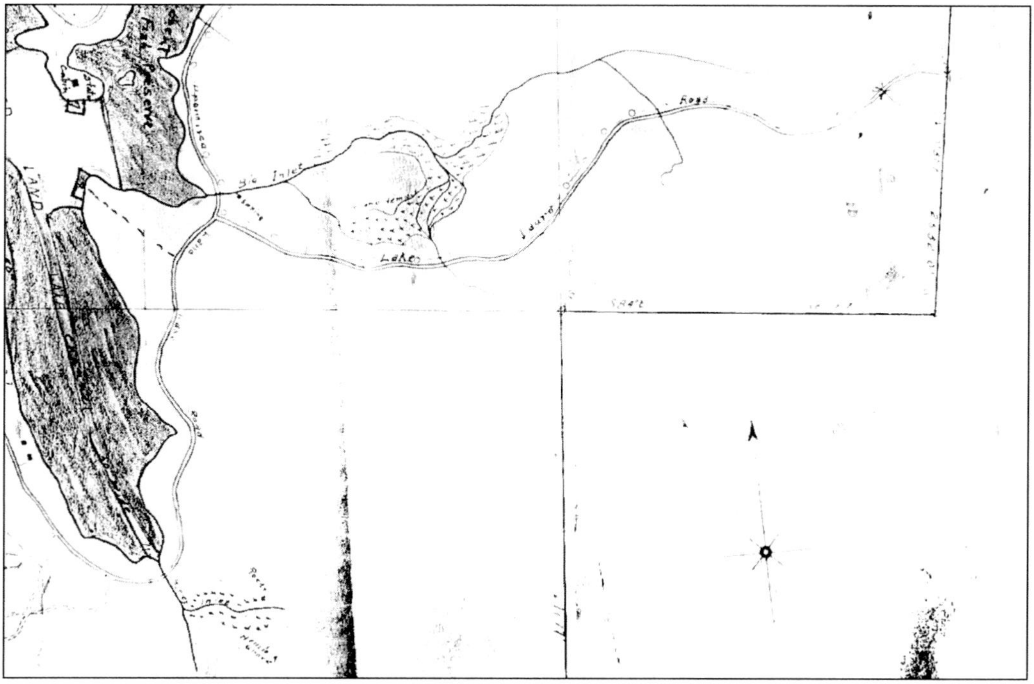

Among the earliest work projects completed was the creation of better roads for the public to use and as access for firefighting. In 1933, the CCC built Lake Laura Road. It provided access to an area in the southwestern corner of the park that was previously inaccessible to forest firefighters. Because it enters private land, it is now closed to the public. (Courtesy Promised Land State Park.)

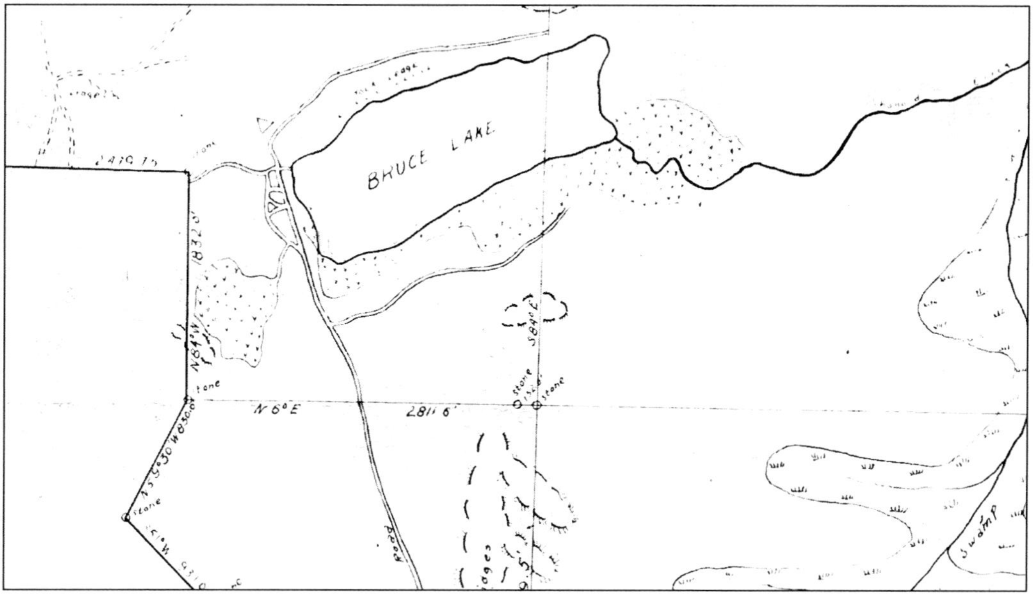

In a land swap with the Blooming Grove Hunting Club in 1930, the park acquired Bruce Lake, previously known as Root's Pond. During the CCC era, the state considered building camping and picnicking facilities around the lake, but after consideration, plans were cancelled and only an access road was built. The area was set aside as the first Natural Wilderness Area in the state. (Courtesy Promised Land State Park.)

The Bruce Lake Road, shown here, was three miles in length and was built by the CCC in 1935, completing a project that had been proposed as a fire suppression measure and to allow public access into that part of the park property. The road reaches the northern end of the glacial lake. (Courtesy Promised Land State Park.)

The Egypt Meadows Road was built at the same time as Bruce Lake Road. Both roads were joined by the Panther Swamp Road. Also, Pickerel Point and Burley Inlet roads and the road around Conservation Island were all built by the CCC. The North Shore Road from Ridgefield Point to Pickerel Point was also finished and completed a loop around Promised Land Lake. (Courtesy Peter Osborne.)

After a survey crew laid out the proposed route, road gangs came in to build it. Road building throughout the park required the moving of tons of rock and providing a finished surface. Large amounts of dynamite were used to blast rock. While the roads have been improved in the years since their construction, the basic designs remain the same. (Courtesy Promised Land State Park.)

Enrollees dressed or finished the roads and also the shoulders. Some of the park's roads would ultimately be blacktopped by the state. Where there had once been no access or rugged logging roads, there were now touring roads for park visitors. The building of roads was considered to be among the toughest of jobs in the CCC. From this hard work came their motto—We Can Take It! (Courtesy Promised Land State Park.)

New parking areas were created at convenient places along the park's roads to accommodate the growing number of visitors and their cars. Culverts for drainage were also built by the CCC boys, and guardrails were installed. (Courtesy Promised Land State Park.)

In the end, the CCC built 30 miles of new roads in and near the park and maintained 28 miles of roadways. During the winter months, CCC boys helped keep the roads in the park clear of snow. (Courtesy Promised Land State Park.)

The CCC boys undertook a number of timber stand improvement projects at Promised Land. Inventories were taken that gave a better picture of the tree stock and soils on the property. They collected seeds for future use and planted 180,000 spruce, red pine, and hemlock seedlings. On average, a CCC boy could plant 400 trees per day. Blister rust control projects were also completed. (Courtesy Promised Land State Park.)

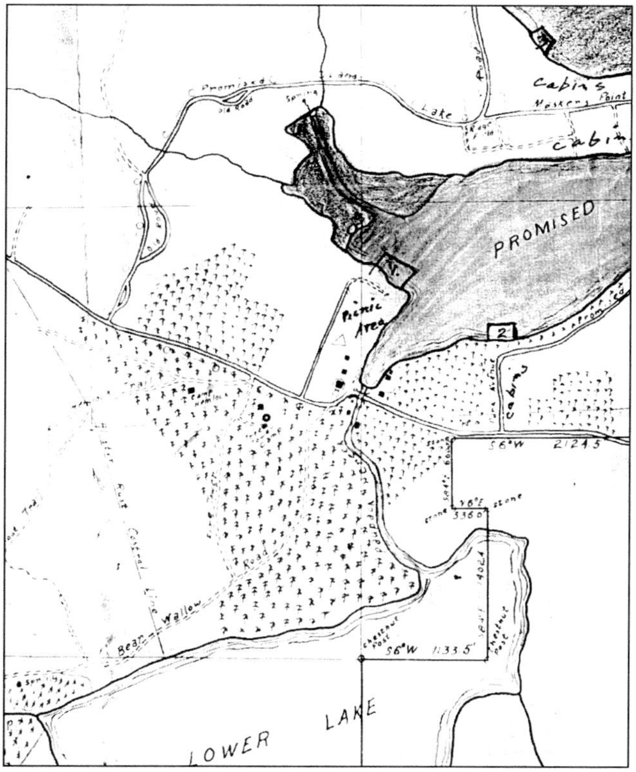

A national catastrophe that also impacted the park was the chestnut blight that killed 4.1 billion trees across the country. Dead, injured, and diseased trees were removed along all of the roads to prevent forest fires. Hundreds of truckloads of brush were burned, eliminating a major fire hazard. Brush shelters were built, which also encouraged the return of wildlife, and feed was distributed in the park. (Courtesy Promised Land State Park.)

The enrollees thinned out forests and cut up dead wood, which was used as split rails, telephone poles, lumber, and firewood for campers. The success of Camp Pocono and many other camps with their forestry projects gave the CCC the nickname of the "Roosevelt Tree Army." (Courtesy Promised Land State Park.)

CCC boys continue to plant trees in Promised Land. Here, Tom Frantz, a former CCC foreman, and Conservation Volunteer Robbie McClelland plant a young sapling next to the remains of a tree that a CCC boy planted in the 1930s. Today those CCC trees are mature and are recognizable because they are planted in rows. By 1940, more than half of Pike County's land was reforested. (Courtesy Peter Osborne.)

Certificate of Competency

C.C.C. CAMP S-139
GREENTOWN, PA.

John Stromela

The above named has received a minimum of 8 hours of fire training during the SPRING ~~FALL~~ of 1941 and is certified as a fire fighter.

G. M. INSCOE, SUPERINTENDENT   S. W. CAMPBELL, FORESTER

Some of the most important forestry jobs that CCC boys performed were fighting fires in the region and preemptive work like combating insects and disease and holding firefighting drills. The roads they built not only created access for the public but also were used for firefighting and firebreaks. There were at least three fires at Camp Pocono during the time of its existence, and three buildings with tools were destroyed. (Courtesy Promised Land State Park.)

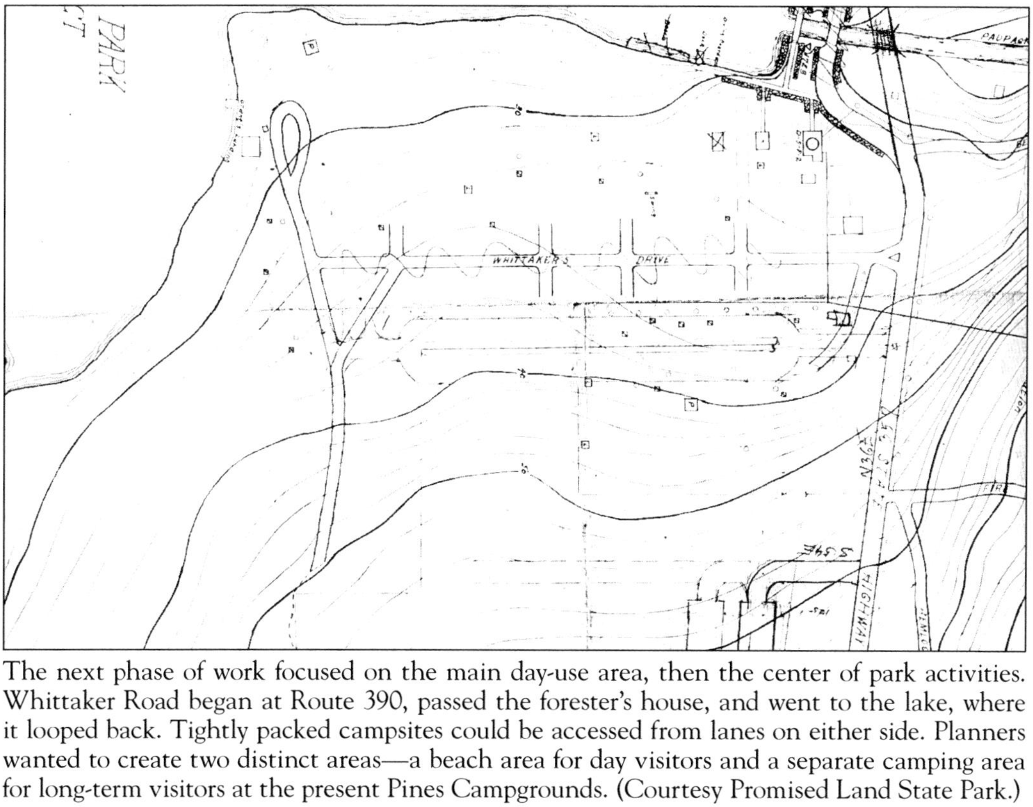

The next phase of work focused on the main day-use area, then the center of park activities. Whittaker Road began at Route 390, passed the forester's house, and went to the lake, where it looped back. Tightly packed campsites could be accessed from lanes on either side. Planners wanted to create two distinct areas—a beach area for day visitors and a separate camping area for long-term visitors at the present Pines Campgrounds. (Courtesy Promised Land State Park.)

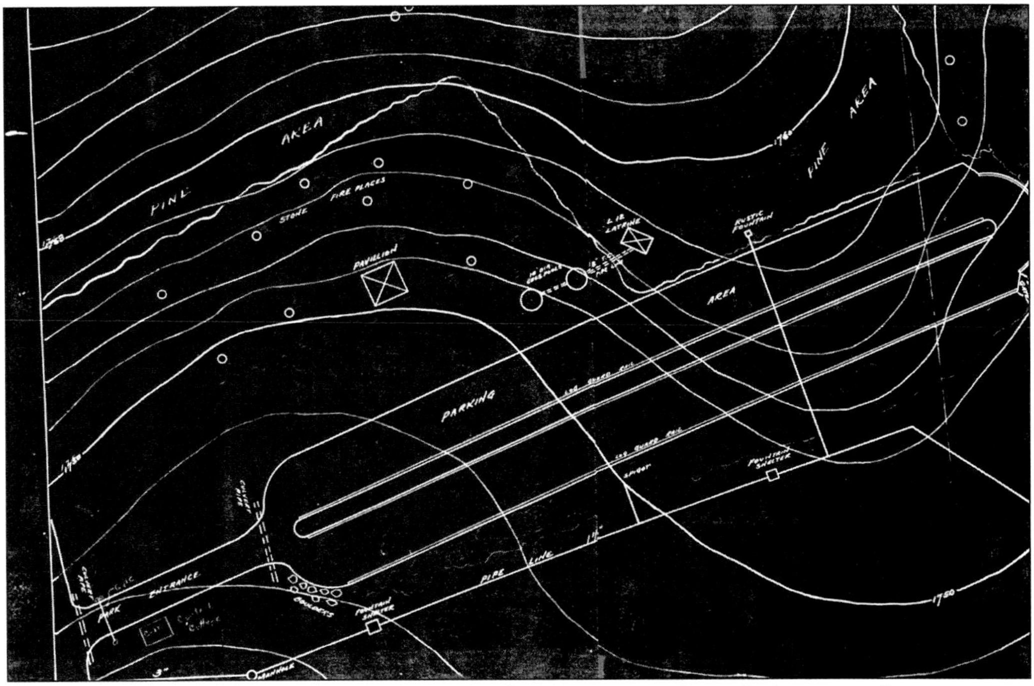

During the late 1930s, the former campground area was transformed. A new parking area was constructed that created an island in the middle for unique plantings. A bathhouse and large pavilion were built, along with several shelters. A water distribution system utilizing a reservoir along with rustic stone water fountains was erected as well as comfort stations. Sports fields, picnic tables, and fireplaces were added, along with a new beach with walkways. (Courtesy Promised Land State Park.)

The bathhouse was located near the main beach along with a new boat dock. Here, CCC boys take a rest on the stone steps as they near completion of the project. Many of the young men in the CCC had never done manual labor before their enlistment. By the time the boys left the CCC, they were proficient in the use of hand tools. (Courtesy Promised Land State Park.)

This 1950s view of the bathhouse is from the back side of the building. The ladies' room was on the left, the mens' room was on the right, and a concession stand was located in the central part of the structure. The bathhouse was used until 1978, when it was razed and replaced with a concrete block structure in the same location. (Courtesy Pennsylvania State Archives.)

A new pavilion, located between the forester's house and bathhouse, was constructed between 1938 and 1939 using big timbers and stone. The pavilion was a hallmark of the style of design that has come to be known as "parkitecture". A pre-CCC pavilion, which was destroyed by fire in the early 1960s, was located near the entrance to the day-use parking area. (Courtesy Promised Land State Park.)

The surviving pavilion remains one of the most architecturally significant buildings in the park. Designs used by the CCC were usually generated at a local level, although generic designs were provided by the United States Forest Service. In 1958, the picnic shelter was enclosed and was utilized as a concession stand. In 2002, the alterations were removed and it was restored to its original appearance. (Courtesy David Heiney.)

A structure that has long elicited interest by park visitors is the stone tower across from the main day-use area entrance on Route 390. Constructed by the CCC in 1938, the incinerator was used to burn garbage generated by the park's visitors. Trucks drove up a lane behind the structure and dumped their garbage in from the top to be burned. (Courtesy David Heiney.)

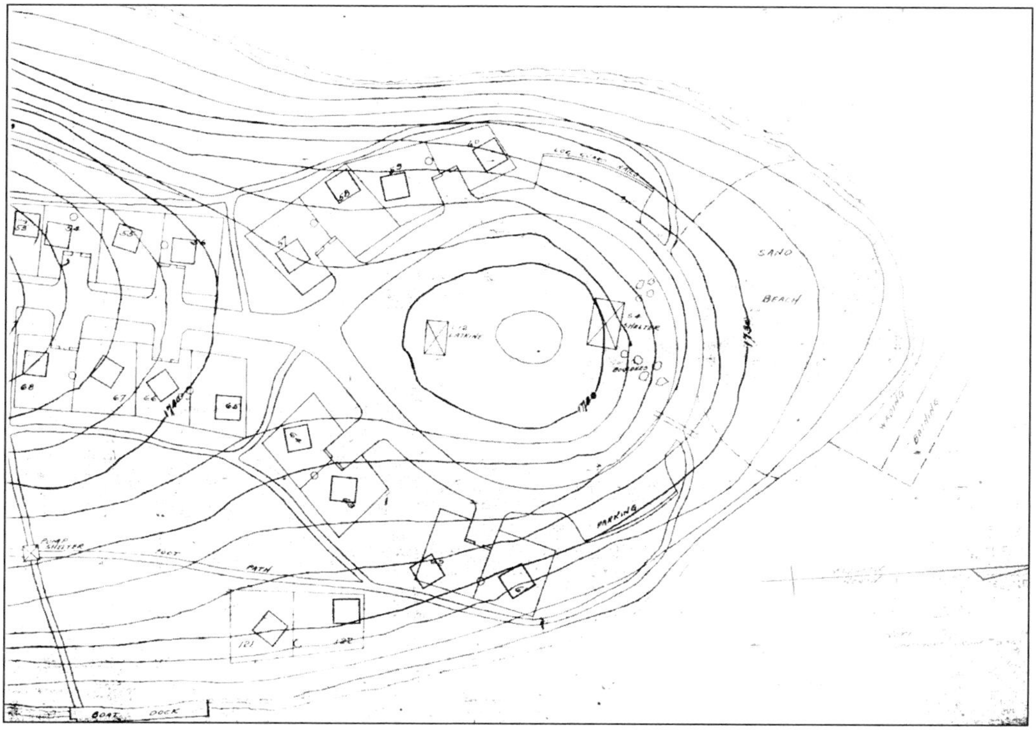

In 1936, plans for more than 100 campsites at the Pines were discarded and instead relocated at Pickerel Point. Soon, CCC boys were at work building the new camping facility. Camping at the very end of Pickerel Point, previously known as Dewey Point, had predated the CCC. (Courtesy Promised Land State Park.)

The new Pickerel Point campgrounds were quickly utilized. Work included pit latrines, campsites, tent platforms, and hand pumps for water. Wells were drilled using drilling equipment that was shared by the district foresters. Temporary campgrounds were also built at Burley Inlet, Ridgefield Point, and Snow Shanty Run. (Courtesy Promised Land State Park.)

Company 1399 modernized and enlarged the pit latrines and built 40 new fireplaces and 80 tables. The campgrounds along Whittaker Road that had been established in 1925 were closed. With the opening of Pickerel Point, new traditions developed for visitors, and it became a favorite of campers. (Courtesy Promised Land State Park.)

As part of the complex at Pickerel Point, the CCC built this handsome shelter. It was constructed into an embankment at the end of the point and stood until the 1980s. After the CCC built a new boat dock, Henry Masker built another road and moved his boat concession to Pickerel Point. He also built a new parking area after World War II. (Courtesy Len and Lucille Martin.)

In addition to the shelter, the CCC built a new beach at the point. Sand was placed on the ice in the late winter of 1940, and in the spring, the sand sank to the bottom of the lake, creating the beautiful new beach. With the completion of all the new facilities, hundreds of campers could be found at the park on a given summer day. (Courtesy Promised Land State Park.)

Another goal of the designers was to accommodate those who might not be willing to have such an intimate experience with the outdoors. For them, the CCC built 12 overnight cabins along Bear Wallow Road between 1937 and 1938, including this one, No. 11. The park's plan had originally called for 24. (Courtesy Pennsylvania State Archives.)

The cabins were furnished with a dining table, chairs, wooden benches, sleeping quarters, and kitchen equipment. The buildings also have a handsome porch and fireplace; they remain a favorite destination for park visitors. Even today, they retain their original furnishings and must be reserved months in advance during the summer and fall seasons. (Courtesy Jack Cressman.)

The CCC's work included making numerous improvements to Promised Land Lake. In 1932, the earthen dam that created the lake began to leak and a new concrete core dam was built by the Department of Forests and Waters. To enhance the appearance of the newly constructed dam, the CCC lined the western side of the dam with stone to give it the rustic look that it has today. (Courtesy Promised Land State Park.)

A sluiceway, pictured on the right side of the lake's dam, was added to lower the lake and to allow for a continual water flow into the east branch of the Wallenpaupack Creek. The CCC also built a wooden footbridge across the spillway, which created a handsome aesthetic feature. The lake now covers more than 400 acres and measures 15 feet at its deepest point. (Courtesy Robert Koehler.)

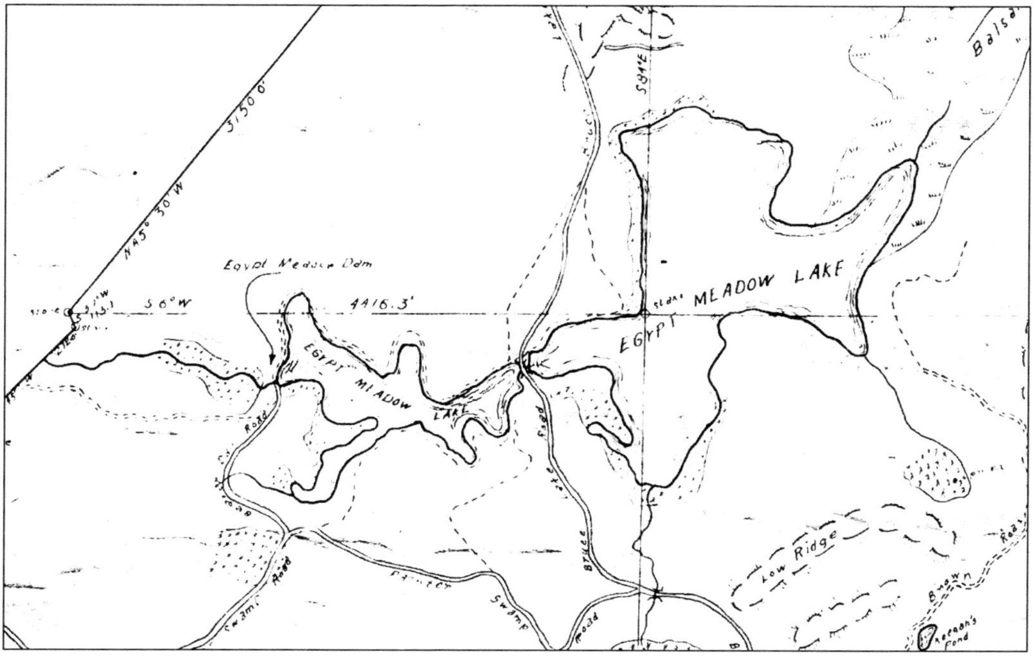

As part of the state's strategy to provide visitors with lake facilities, it was determined that a lake could be created in the Balsam Swamp, where a man-made lake had previously been built in 1839 for a sawmill and then breached in 1860. To get to the proposed Egypt Meadows Lake, a new road was constructed from Route 390 that continued on to Bruce Lake. (Courtesy Promised Land State Park.)

The Egypt Meadow Lake was created in 1935 by the CCC when two dams were constructed, including this spillway that helped to control the height of the lake. Any overflowing water coursed over bluestone rip-rap that was placed on end. Wooden boards could be added or removed to adjust the water level. (Courtesy Peter Osborne.)

A second, larger dam with a spillway was built. The dam is 200-feet long, 22-feet wide, 14-feet high, and built with bluestone. When completed, the lake was 150 acres in size and was stocked with pickerel and panfish. Today this beautiful and popular lake is only accessible by foot and remains a scenic fishing spot. (Courtesy Peter Osborne.)

Many of the hiking trails that continue to be used today were also built by the CCC . They built 12 miles of footpaths. Much of the labor required of the CCC boys was hard and physically demanding. The enrollees wore out a lot of equipment including shovels, picks, and digging bars. Trail construction required moving rocks to provide a stable hiking surface and new footbridges. (Courtesy Promised Land State Park.)

The CCC was also responsible for a variety of other projects, including the installation of telephone lines, the construction of signs, the demolition of undesirable structures, the development of stream and wildlife projects, and the handling of emergencies. They maintained the park's boundaries, created maps, and built a garage for Whittaker Lodge. Even as the CCC boys were working in the park, visitors began to use the facilities as soon as they became available. (Courtesy Promised Land State Park.)

As work was going on in the park, CCC boys were working in the surrounding state forest. In 1934, they built the White Deer Lake Road around White Deer Lake. They also worked at the Owego Ranger Station completing landscaping projects and building a new garage and building the Owego Public Campground. The CCC boys built the road to High Knob, on which a fire tower was constructed. (Courtesy Peter Osborne.)

When the CCC left Promised Land in 1941, it was said that it was to be given "due credit for its splendid work in beautifying and making practical use of Promised Land Lake . . . so as to make possible a wider use of nature's playground by the crowded city populace." Many of the projects remain—Egypt Meadow Lake, Pickerel Point campgrounds, the day-use area, roads, trails, and buildings. (Courtesy Promised Land State Park.)

On July 1, 1941, Camp Pocono closed its doors and most of the buildings were demolished. About 1,500 men served at Promised Land, and for many, the CCC was the greatest experience in their lives. More than 200,000 man days were worked, and hundreds of thousands of dollars spent during the CCC years, a bargain indeed, especially considering that millions of patrons have visited the park since. (Courtesy Promised Land State Park.)

Most enrollees left the CCC in much better shape than when they arrived. The outdoor life, good food, and hard work made wiser and more mature men of them and in many cases prepared them for an uncertain world. In the decades that followed their work in the camps, they became great advocates for the parks and urged that they be maintained and adequately funded. (Courtesy Promised Land State Park.)

By 1940, fewer men were signing up for the CCC because of better paying jobs in the defense industry. When Pearl Harbor was attacked, America focused on winning the war. About 75 percent of the men who served in the CCC served in World War II. President Roosevelt had hoped that 5,000 CCC camps would be maintained permanently after the war, but it was not to be. (Courtesy Minisink Valley Historical Society.)

Five

The People's Park

During World War II, park use declined dramatically. However, in the years following the war, the park witnessed a continued expansion of its facilities, increased visitation, and the acquisition of Lower Lake. An important omen for the future took place in 1955, when Maurice Goddard was appointed Secretary of the Department of Forests and Waters. Goddard developed a plan to build a state park within 25 miles of every Pennsylvania resident. The study proposed 175 new parks. In the same year, Gov. George Leader also signed legislation using oil and gas revenues from wells on state land to be used towards conservation and land acquisition.

In the early 1960s, Goddard proposed two new state programs, Project 70 and Project 500, creating new momentum to build on the work of the early park developers and the CCC. Project 70, a statewide effort to spend $70 million, increased the number of parks and also had the effect of promoting additional development of the state parks. Project 500, proposed in 1968, allowed additional funding for recreational facilities and environmental projects.

In the 1990s, this interest was renewed as more projects began as Key 93 funding was initiated. More recently, there have been two other initiatives, Growing Greener I and II, which have also expanded on those earlier efforts. As a result of state-wide initiatives over the last four decades, Promised Land State Park has been enlarged and improved and the number of state parks in Pennsylvania has doubled.

When the park was created, there were two large privately owned tracts within it. These parcels, separate from each other, make up the majority of the village of Promised Land. The village developed as the park's visitation increased, and the business community benefited from the park. While not within the park's jurisdiction, the village is, for residents and park visitors alike, very much a part of the park experience. (Courtesy Erwin Weber.)

The village provides ambulance services, volunteer fire protection, lodging, food, gasoline, and camping supplies and is home to several civic organizations. The Promised Land Civic Association was created to promote community pride. The Promised Land Sportsman's Association provides hunter safety demonstrations and stocks fish in Paupack Creek. It also sponsors activities related to hunting and fishing, including fishing contests and youth scholarships. (Courtesy Dale Edwards.)

Two churches have served park visitors and nearby residents, one is the Promised Land Protestant Community Church. The congregation was founded in 1951. In 1954, the church was constructed; it opened to worshipers in 1955. (Courtesy Jack Cressman.)

The second church, now called Our Lady of Fatima Mission, Roman Catholic Church of St. Bernadette, was built in 1951 and also serves both full and part time residents during the summer months. (Courtesy Jack Cressman.)

In 1947, the highway bridge located next to the Promised Land Lake dam was removed, and the dangerous curve in the highway was straightened. A new bridge was built; an added benefit was that passers-by had a better view of the dam. Remnants of the old road can still be seen between the dam and the new bridge. (Courtesy Peter Osborne.)

Visitation at the park continued to rise because of an increase in the population, improvements in transportation, a growing recreation industry, construction of new highways, increased incomes, and more leisure time. This increased demand and, along with the Goddard initiatives, led to the construction of a number of new facilities. Here, "bathing beauties" (as they are described on the post card) are enjoying themselves at the public beach. (Courtesy Promised Land State Park.)

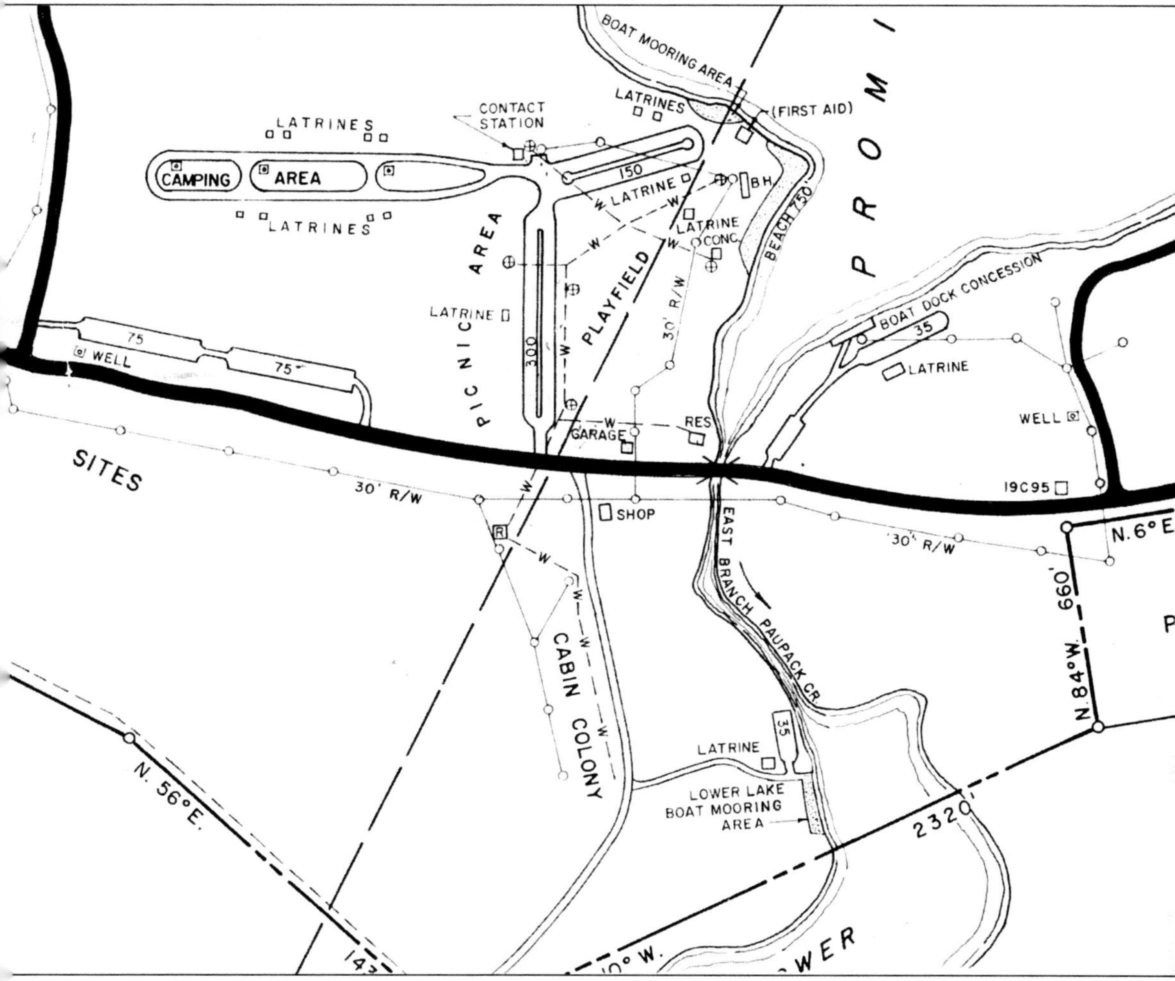

After the war, park officials looked again at plans for a campground facility near the pine plantation to handle the increasing number of visitors. In the late 1940s, campgrounds were constructed at the edge of the pines, based on the CCC's original plan, and opened in 1950. The campsites were separate from the beach area, but close enough to walk to. New parking facilities were added to serve the increasing number of vehicles and give the area its present configuration. (Courtesy Promised Land State Park.)

With the opening of the Pines Campgrounds, campers would stay all summer within a short walk to the beach. The white pine plantation, originally planted in 1912, with its majestic trees, became home to a new generation of campers, as camping in "the Pines" became a new tradition. Pictured here is Richard Deck reading to his children and his wife, Edith (center), in 1948. (Courtesy Pennsylvania State Archives.)

Long-time visitors remember the contact station, which controlled access to the Pines Campground. In the late 1950s, Jimmy and Debbie Wells had their picture taken in front of the building where the park's rangers worked. Debbie is now the park's administrative assistant. The building has been moved several times: first to Pickerel Point, then to its current location in the maintenance yard. (Courtesy Ginny Wells.)

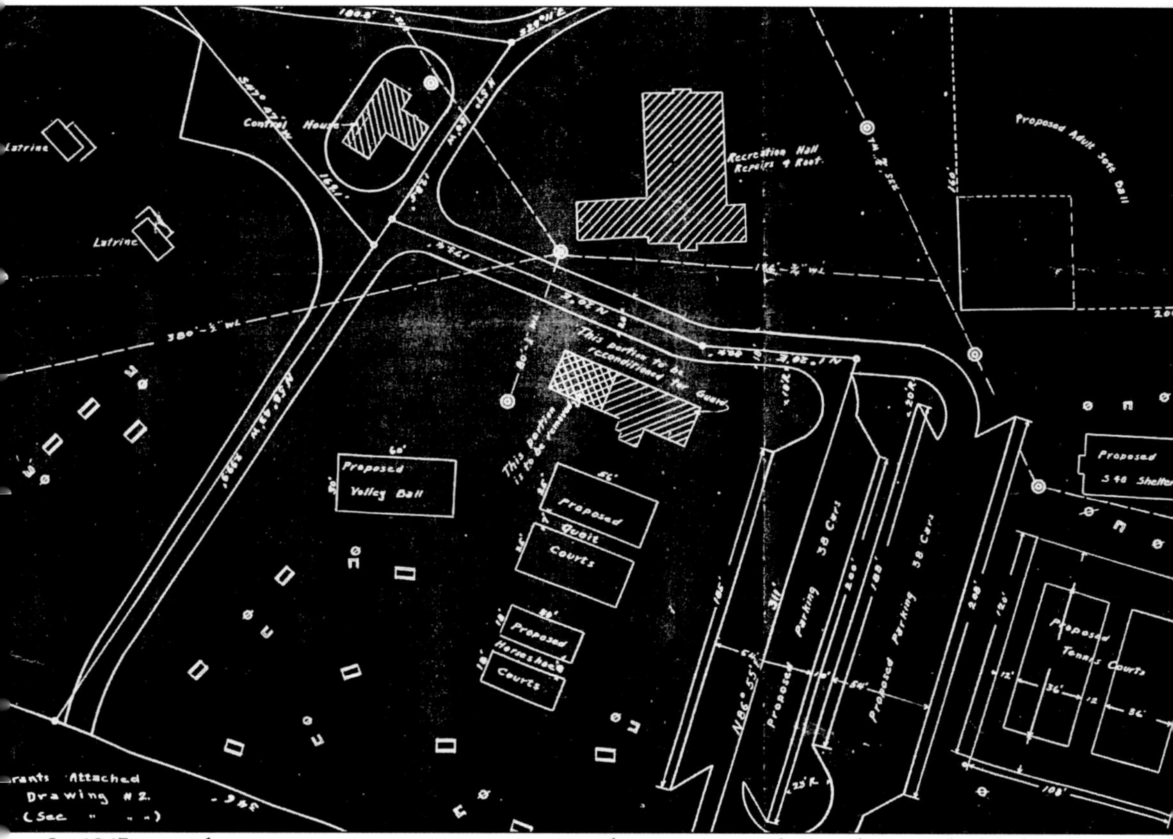

In 1947, consideration was given to creating a new day-use area at the southern end of Pickerel Point. This area would have included a softball field and sports facilities, shelters, latrines, and additional campsites; it would have utilized several of the remaining CCC buildings. In the end, the proposal was never implemented. It was during this time that park management considered reducing the number of long-term campers, people who had previously stayed the whole summer at the same campsite. After considerable controversy, all long-term camping was ended in the park by 1964. (Courtesy Promised Land State Park.)

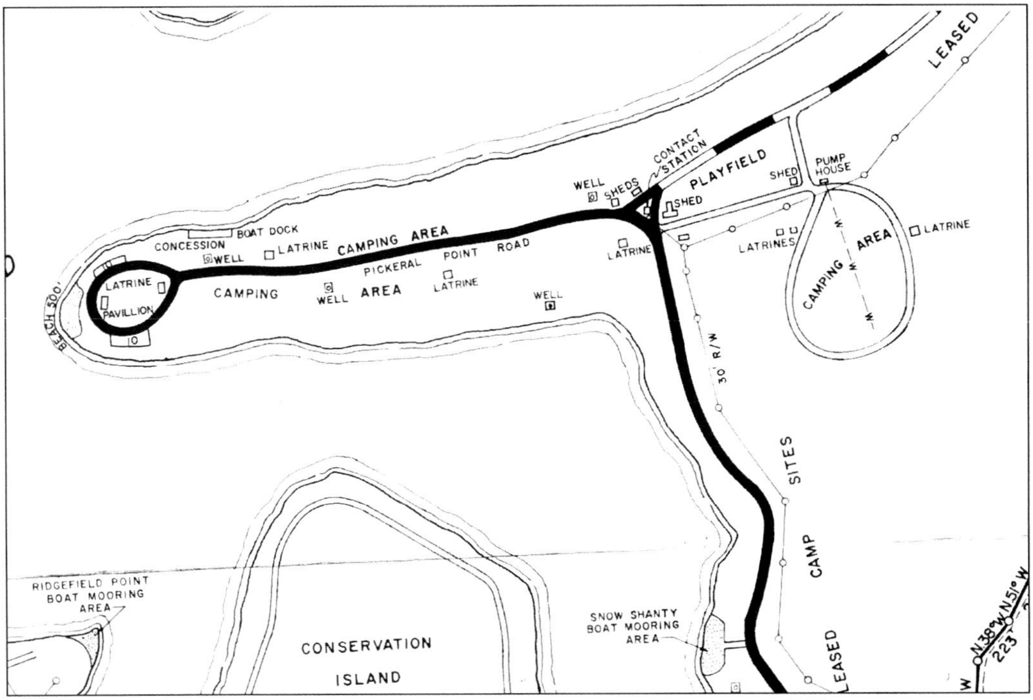

After the plans for a day-use area at Pickerel Point were scrapped, the Deerfield Camping Area was built and opened in 1956. The Deerfield facilities were improved in 1976, with the construction of a new comfort station and a dumping station. (Courtesy Promised Land State Park.)

In the early 1950s, a beautiful stone arch bridge was built, connecting Conservation Island to the mainland. The island was known in an earlier time as Goat Island because it was home to a herd of goats owned by a local farmer who reached the island by crossing a plank causeway. Later, it was called Pyle Island, after the well-known district forester, E. C. Pyle. (Courtesy Peter Osborne.)

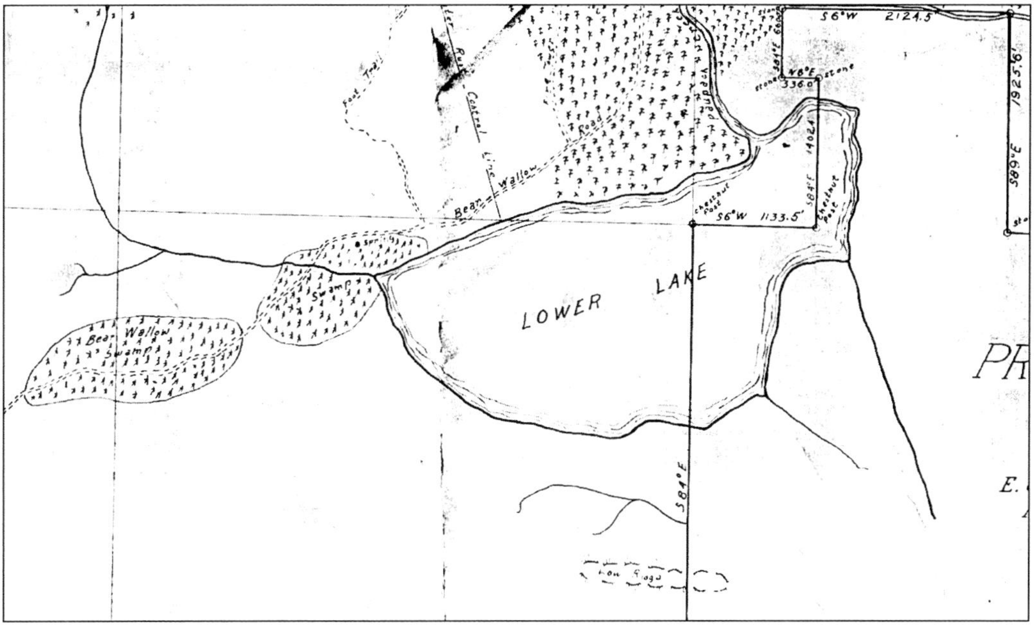

Lower Lake is believed to have been created by a stone dam that was built by Horace Kipp for a sawmill at the narrows, east of the present dam. The size and shape of the small lake changed regularly depending on water levels. In 1947, the commonwealth acquired the land around the lake that it did not already own and began to consider plans for new facilities. (Courtesy Promised Land State Park.)

In 1958, construction began on a substantial earthen dam, replacing an old impoundment further to the east. This enlarged the Lower Lake to 173 acres. Construction was completed in 1959, and the lake opened for use in 1961. A new boat launch area, which included a parking lot and latrine, was built in 1962. Additional work was done on the dam in 1963. (Courtesy Peter Osborne.)

With Lower Lake development underway, the park's activities shifted away from the area around the dam. The park's headquarters and maintenance area were moved to a new location on Route 390 at the southwestern corner of the park. Between 1962 and 1963, a new park office was built in the popular A-frame style. Today the building is used as the ranger's headquarters. The maintenance building behind it was constructed between 1970 and 1971. (Courtesy Promised Land State Park.)

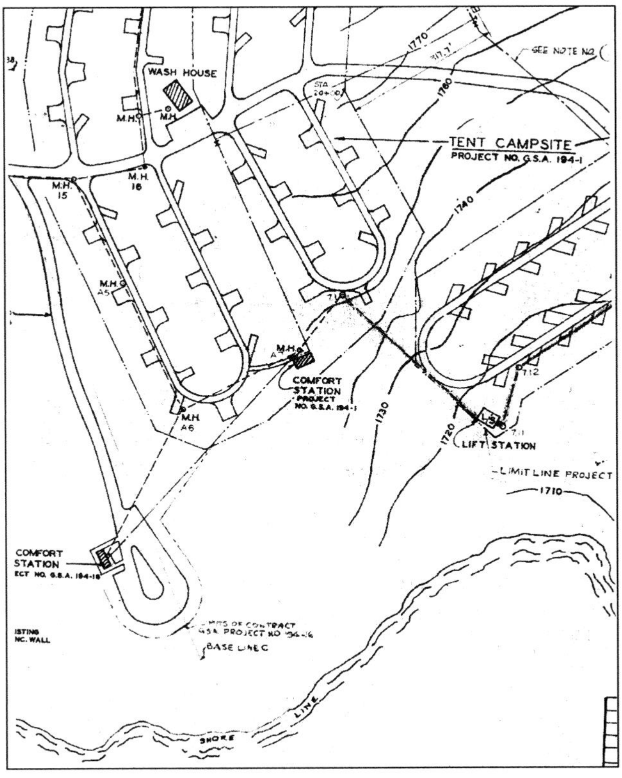

Beginning in 1965 and continuing until 1975, the entire Lower Lake Campground complex was constructed. It included 235 campsites in four separate areas (Beechwood, Northwood, Rhododendron, and Hemlock Hill), four washhouses, two comfort stations, a contact station, a dumping station, new underground electric service, a new bathing beach area, and a public boat launch. It opened on July 6, 1974, having cost almost $2 million. (Courtesy Promised Land State Park.)

As part of the Lower Lake project, and with Project 70 funding, the park constructed new water and sewer facilities. In 1972, a new water tower at Lower Lake was erected. A central sewer system near the Lower Lake facilities, with a handling capacity of up to 200,000 gallons of effluent a day, was also built. (Courtesy Peter Osborne.)

The comfort stations that were built for the four camping areas at Lower Lake served the public until 2005, when they were demolished to make way for more modern and accessible facilities. Just as the Pines Campgrounds and Pickerel Point Campgrounds had before it, the Lower Lake facilities soon became very popular with campers. (Courtesy Promised Land State Park.)

During the 1970s and early 1980s, new renovations and upgrades began around the park and in the day-use area at the main beach to replace aging facilities no longer able to handle the growing number of visitors. A second water tower was constructed, and roads, boat ramps, and parking lots were all blacktopped. (Courtesy Promised Land State Park.)

Until 1962, there had been two boat concessionaires operating at different locations, one at Pickerel Point and the other at the main beach area. After that, one concessionaire took over both. This arrangement remained in place until the 1980s, when the two concessions were consolidated into the present location. This building is on the site of the original Wilson Landing. (Courtesy David Heiney.)

During the late 1970s, new comfort stations were added at the Pines and the day-use area and modern baths were constructed along Bear Wallow Road. The CCC-era bathhouse station and concession stand were razed in 1978, and the bathhouse was built on the same location in 1980. Recently, the cinder-block building was completely refurbished and covered with rough-cut wood siding to give it a rustic appearance. (Courtesy Peter Osborne.)

To meet the demands of an increasingly complex operation in the 1990s, the present park office was built and centralized all administrative and environmental education staff in one location. It is located on Route 390 and just a short distance from the A-frame building. The office was dedicated in a ceremony attended by Lt. Gov. Mark Schweiker. A new park manager's residence was also built in 1995. (Courtesy Peter Osborne.)

A new concession stand was constructed in 2002 on the location of a late 1970s comfort station that was located near the beach area. (Courtesy Peter Osborne.)

In more recent years, projects have been undertaken that have utilized a rustic style evocative of the CCC era. In the tradition of excellent workmanship, the park's staff constructed a new pavilion in the day-use area in 2000. Comfort stations around the park built in the 1970s and 1980s have been sheathed with wood siding to give them a more rustic appearance. (Courtesy David Heiney.)

The park has had a long relationship with young people working within its boundaries since the days of the CCC. In the 1970s, two federally funded youth agencies were created that undertook projects in parks across the country. They were the Youth Conservation Corps (YCC) (1973–present), and the Young Adult Conservation Corps (YACC) (1979–1982). Both agencies were dramatically curtailed in 1981, although the YCC still fulfills its mission. The YCC provided day jobs, while the YACC was a residential program employing young people who were between 16 and 23 years of age. Participants generally upgraded the park's facilities and performed deferred maintenance projects, visitor services, and environmental projects. They also built the Little Falls Trail. (Courtesy Pocono Ridge YCC.)

Another youth agency, the Pennsylvania Conservation Corps (PCC), was formed in 1984 by the Pennsylvania Department of Labor. Young people in this program have worked at various natural resource and cultural projects across the state. The participants are between the ages of 18 and 25. At Promised Land, they helped to convert the former CCC washhouse into an auditorium for park programs and assisted with the construction of the park's present headquarters. Pictured are Department of Conservation and Natural Resources (DCNR) managers and members of the PCC. On the left is Leo Davidovich, then Promised Land's assistant park manager and the park's manager in 2005. Second from left is R. James Grabbe, former assistant regional manager, and third from the right is PCC crew leader Mike Dassance. The other three unidentified young people were members of the Promised Land PCC crew. (Courtesy Promised Land State Park.)

Six

Promised Land State Park Today

If one was to ask visitors, cabin owners, park officials, land managers, and historians to describe Promised Land State Park today, one would get a variety of descriptions. The visitor's perception of the park's size is very different from what it actually is. Most visitors would probably guess that Promised Land extends far beyond its present boundaries into forestland that is now actually part of the Delaware State Forest, and which totals 12,464 acres.

Most visitors are probably not aware of which agency manages the land, or how it is administered. They are here to hike; camp; have a picnic; go boating, swimming, or fishing on the lakes; or just traverse on nicely designed roads and trails. While annual visitation varies from year to year, the average number of visitors for the last 10 years is 402,000. Since the 1950s, the highest estimated count was 1,052,577 in 1989—the lowest estimated count was 264,242 in 1958.

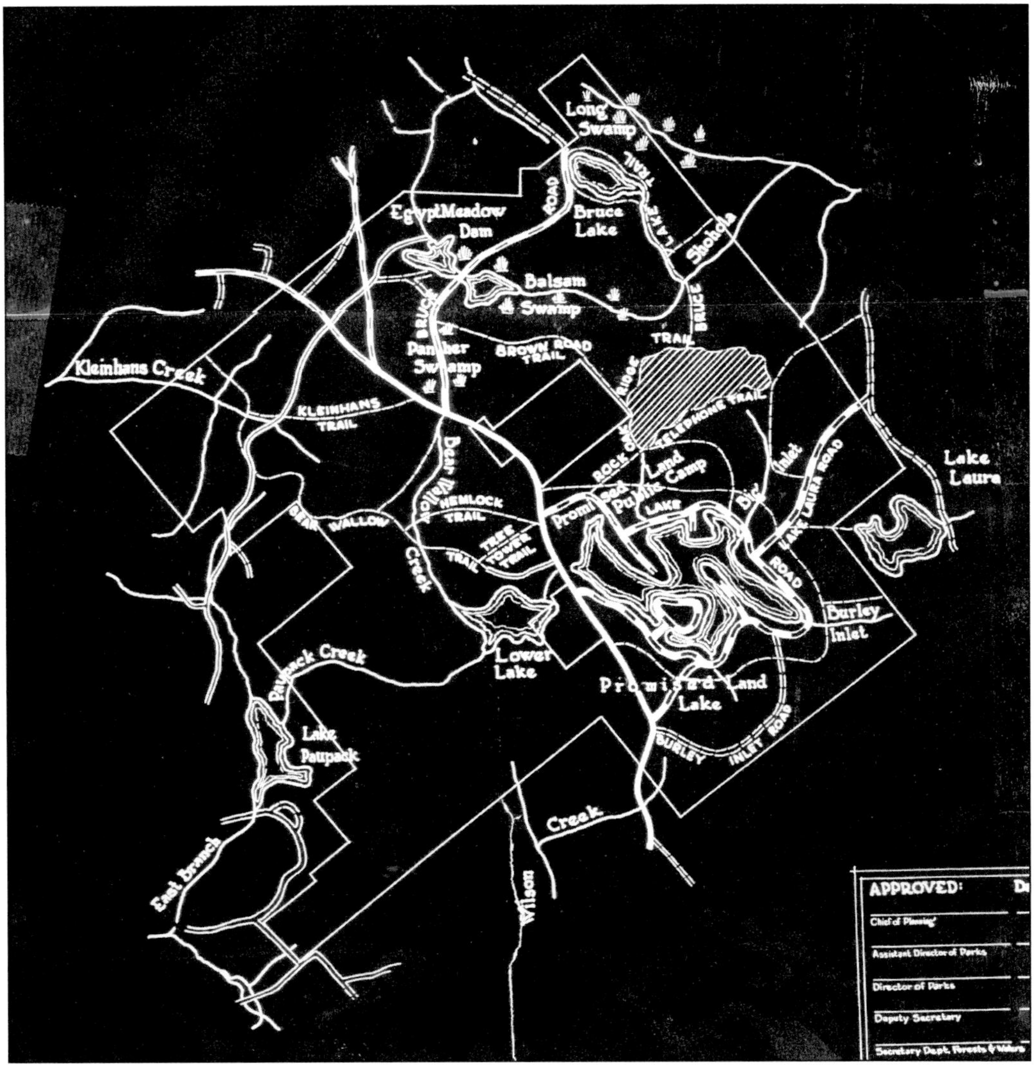

With the beginning of land acquisitions in 1898, Promised Land State Park grew in size. Since those early years, Promised Land has evolved as the government agencies charged with maintaining and running the forests and parks have themselves been realigned and purposes changed. These realignments have brought about regular changes in the park's operations. (Courtesy Promised Land State Park.)

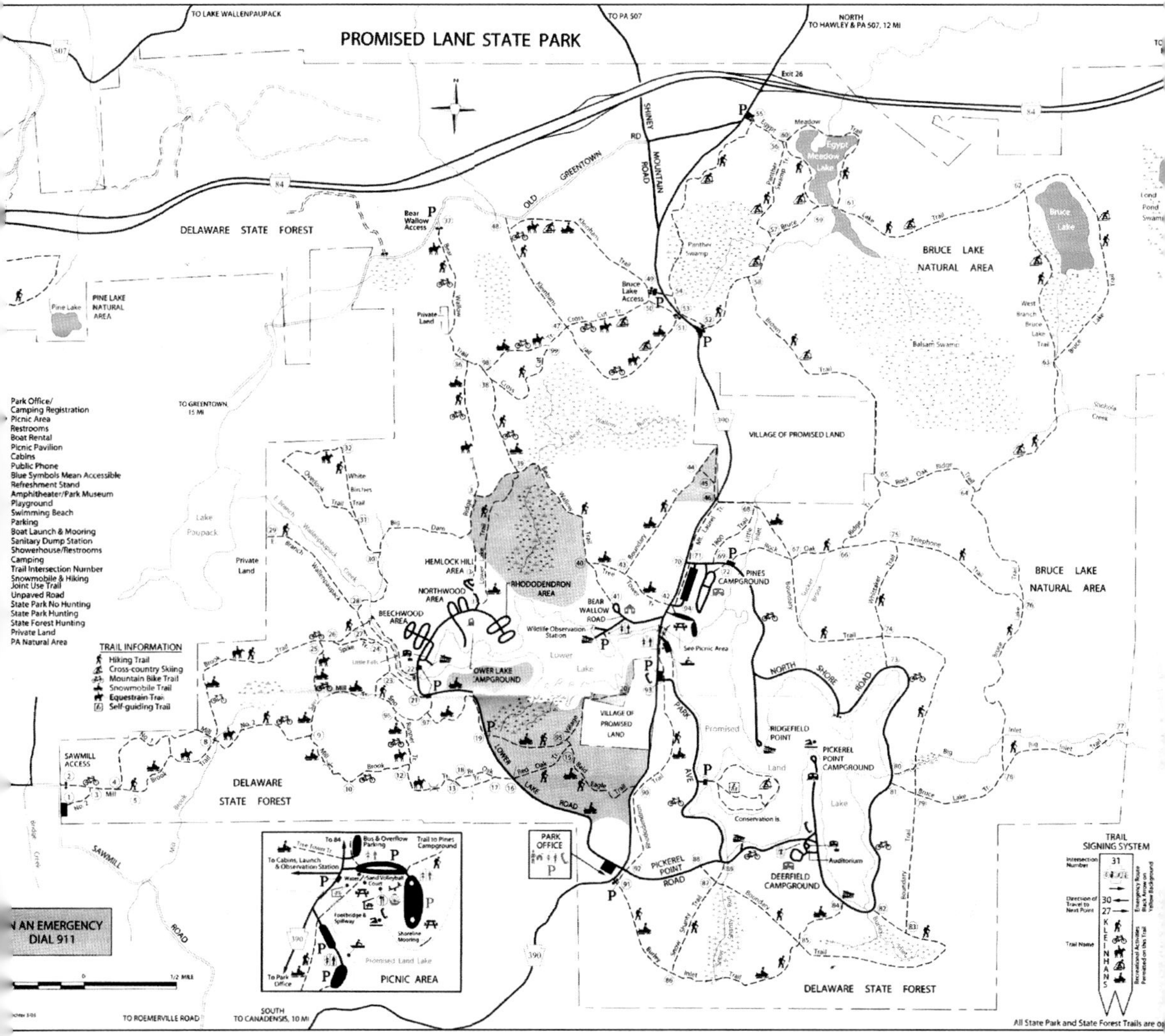

Today the park controls 2,970 acres, although the surrounding acreage is still owned by the commonwealth. This map shows the current Promised Land State Park boundaries along with the surrounding Delaware State Forest. Of particular note is the Bruce Lake Natural Area, which was included in Promised Land's jurisdiction for 61 of the last 76 years. Also, parts of Lower Lake have been within, and then taken out of, the park's official administrative boundaries. Today the lake is entirely within the park's jurisdiction as it has been since the campgrounds were constructed. (Courtesy Promised Land State Park.)

An important development in creating better access to Promised Land was the construction of Interstate Route 84 beginning in 1968. The highway allowed visitors to get to the park more easily. However, it also impacted one of the most remote features of the park, Bruce Lake, where traffic noise can now be heard. Interstate 80 and the Northeast extension of the Pennsylvania Turnpike also make the park more accessible. (Courtesy Peter Osborne.)

Fishing has remained one of the most popular activities in the park since 1905. Both lakes contain a diverse array of species and Lower Lake has been stocked with trout since 1994. There are limits on the take; perch and pickerel can be caught in both lakes. A Pennsylvania fishing license is required to fish at the park. (Courtesy Promised Land State Park.)

Fishing is a great activity for family members of different generations. There are also several streams at Promised Land where fly fisherman can ply their trade. This includes the scenic east branch of the Wallenpaupack Creek, a favorite for anglers with its excellent trout fishing. (Courtesy David Heiney.)

Swimming has long been a popular activity during the summer months. There are two public beaches, one at the day-use area and the second at Pickerel Point. Thousands partake of the clear waters of Promised Land Lake, now 422 acres in size. (Courtesy Promised Land State Park.)

On a hot, humid weekend day or holiday, the beach at the day-use area can be packed with hundreds of visitors and campers. Today more than 400,000 visitors come to the park annually. On an average day, 50 percent of the visitors to the park are from Pennsylvania. On a busy weekend, 3,000 visitors are using the resources that a small township might require. (Courtesy Promised Land State Park.)

Water sports remain popular; there are six boat launches available for visitors and a concessionaire that rents boats to the public. Whether it be a 1930s makeshift sailboat like this one or a modern fiberglass kayak, people love to use boats on both lakes. Only electric motors or non-motorized boats are permitted, maintaining the peaceful experience of the lakes. (Courtesy Robert Koehler.)

Today there are four campgrounds with over 400 campsites open for the camping season. One of the campgrounds is open year round. More than 70 percent of the park's overnight visitors are from Pennsylvania; visitors from New Jersey and New York account for another 20 percent. Of the overnight visitors from Pennsylvania, the largest group is from the Lehigh Valley. (Courtesy David Heiney.)

Folding camping trailers, travel trailers, fifth wheel trailers, truck campers, and motor homes have long been a tradition at Promised Land. The earlier trailers were much simpler when compared with today's recreation vehicles. Now, the trailers are longer, wider, and higher. Many have the amenities of a small home on wheels. More than 100 campsites offer electric hookups. (Courtesy Peter Osborne.)

There are 29 miles of hiking trails in the park that can be used by patrons with a range of abilities and interests. The 1800 is a popular trail that was built by park volunteers in 1984, along the 1800 foot contour line. Today visitors occasionally ask for information about the 1-800 trail, as in a toll-free phone number, certainly a sign of the times. (Courtesy David Heiney.)

The park is not only a place to camp, fish, or hike but it is now a frequent host to running races, including this one as a benefit for the Wayne-Pike Chapter of the American Red Cross. Scouting groups have also been involved with the park; local Girl Scouts created a compass course, and Boy Scouts participate in annual clean-ups. (Courtesy Promised Land State Park.)

Although common in its early years, current park visitors are occasionally surprised by an equestrian rider or two passing through the park. Also, park office employees are asked by newlyweds, "What do your bridal trails offer?" not knowing the precise meaning of the term. There are about 12 miles of equestrian trails on adjacent state forest land, which can be accessed through the park. (Courtesy David Heiney.)

Hunters continue to use the park in specific designated hunting areas. Small game, pheasant, turkey, grouse, black bear, and deer can be taken at the appropriate times of the year. Hunting remains a source of food as well as a wildlife management tool in the commonwealth. Pictured here is Donald Heiney with a deer taken in the Promised Land region. (Courtesy David Heiney.)

During the winter months, the park remains a very busy place, as snowmobilers, cross-country skiers, snowshoers, and other winter enthusiasts all come to use the facilities. There are 22 miles of snowmobile trails that are located in the park and adjacent state forest land. (Courtesy Promised Land State Park.)

Another popular winter sport is ice-fishing, when friends and family gather on the ice of both lakes, drill holes, and fish. After that it is a long wait under a small shelter with food and refreshments. Ice-skating and cross-country skiing are also popular winter activities. (Courtesy David Heiney.)

Various kinds of playground equipment, including swings, are available for children in the main day-use area. The park has continued to upgrade its playground equipment so that it conforms to the latest in recreation standards and provides families with young children a place to enjoy the park. The Promised Land Civic Association and park patrons provided some of the funding for the playground equipment. (Courtesy Peter Osborne.)

As part of the growing environmental movement that was sweeping the nation in the 1970s, the first environmental interpretive technician, Dr. Emery Swan, was hired at the park. In 1975, a park museum was opened to the public in the former CCC officers' quarters, which had been leased as a private cabin. Today the staff educates the public about cultural, historical, and natural resources in the park. (Courtesy Promised Land State Park.)

From 1984 to 1985, the park museum underwent major renovations as new exhibits were built on the history of the park, the CCC's role, and natural resources. Behind it, an amphitheater was built. In addition, a new auditorium was created in the old CCC washhouse. The interior was gutted and renovated to include a stage and seating arrangements for use in public programs like this reptile program. (Courtesy Promised Land State Park.)

In 1981, a Volunteers-in-Parks (VIP) program was created at Promised Land. The VIP program's volunteers assisted with a multitude of tasks that enhanced the visitor's experience. In 1989, the VIP program was honored by the commonwealth. Today they are called Conservation Volunteers, and they conduct regularly scheduled programs for visitors, initiate new programs, operate the Masker museum, and help with park activities. (Courtesy Peter Osborne.)

Seven

LOOKING TO THE FUTURE

As the centennial of the opening of Promised Land State Park is celebrated, the commonwealth's parklands remain an oasis for state residents and visitors from the surrounding region alike. Everyone remembers its fascinating history, and as they look to its future, they do so with hope that the original vision of the park will continue. Today the commonwealth's path is directed in its plan called *Shaping A Sustainable Pennsylvania: DCNR's Blueprint for Action*. It calls for preserving the integrity of existing park lands, expanding the environmental education programs, preserving open space, building sustainable communities, and creating partnerships with local and regional communities and organizations.

There are many challenges facing this park and others across the country. Budget shortfalls, natural resources that are threatened, and invasive species are all concerns. Significant historic structures have been lost, and overuse remains another challenge as well as the way people vacation today. There is increasing development underway in the region around the park. Twice since 1905, the park has been witness to major natural disasters.

There are also many successes. Volunteers continue to give thousands of hours of time to augment the park's staff. Donations have been made to undertake projects, most notably the park's museum. The park continues to offer excellent educational programs, upgrade its facilities as funds allow, and provide a quality recreational experience to visitors. The devotion of a century of service by state employees is appreciated by visitors and supporters of the park alike.

The preservation of critical species remains an important priority for the park. In 1999, a pair of bald eagles began nesting at Lower Lake. In all, eleven fledglings have been produced since. The bald eagle, our national symbol, remains on the threatened species list, although the eagle population has made a remarkable comeback in the nearby Delaware and Lackawaxen river valleys. (Courtesy Promised Land State Park.)

A critical problem for the park is the challenge that the natural resources continually face. For example, the wooly adelgid, an insect, is killing hemlock trees throughout the northeastern United States including in the park. Wooly adelgid will alter the park's ecosystem for generations to come. Gypsy moths have periodically ravaged oak trees as they did in 2005. Invasive species, plants not natural to the area, like foxglove, are overwhelming and eliminating the native plants. (Courtesy Promised Land State Park.)

Critical issues facing all of the state's parks and forests are the level of funding needed to operate and enhance them and the decline in the number of staff at each park. During these challenging fiscal times, the park's patrons need to speak with a united voice. The people need to create greater awareness of the park's maintenance and financial needs. If the legislators do not hear from the people, the parks will suffer. (Courtesy Promised Land State Park.)

Another critical issue is the constant maintenance that is required of all the park's facilities, including many buildings and 2,970 acres of park land. Typical of the ongoing maintenance is the work done in 2003 to the dam at the head of Promised Land Lake, which prevented undermining of the dam. Work was also completed on the bypass that allows water to continually flow into the stream below it. (Courtesy Promised Land State Park.)

To accommodate the changing demands of visitors, the park continues to upgrade its facilities. In 2005, major improvements upgrading the campgrounds at Lower Lake were undertaken. When finished, the improvements will cause less erosion, create a smaller human footprint on the forest, enhance the visitor's experience, and make facilities more accessible. Major renovations are also being planned in other campgrounds in the park. (Courtesy Peter Osborne.)

The way people travel today creates dilemmas for the park. In the early 20th century, there were none of the amenities that are now considered necessities. The quiet of the forest is now interrupted by a cell phone, and the darkness is not quite so dark because of the glow of a laptop computer, handheld game, or television, which can be seen or heard in campsites. (Courtesy Harry Leitheiser.)

Another problem is the regular interaction between the park's wildlife and visitors. Bears wander into campsites regularly, and people feed them, breaking park rules. This also creates future problems that sometimes require the removal or destruction of bears. The proliferation of the deer population and the damage they do has also challenged the park's staff. Numerous deer exclosures have been erected to allow for forest regeneration. (Courtesy Promised Land State Park.)

Pike County and the surrounding counties have been experiencing major growth during the last several decades. This will not impact the park directly because it is almost completely surrounded by Delaware State Forest land and the Bruce Lake Natural Area. In this regard the park is fortunate because visitors' experiences in many other state and national parks across the country are being threatened by development. (Courtesy Peter Osborne.)

Local residents and long-time visitors have a vested interest in the operation of the park, and in many cases, local businesses benefit directly from the park. However, on several occasions, residents and visitors alike have protested proposed projects, such as the demolition of the old ranger station. Another loss was the removal of the Pickerel Point shelter. Two of the support foundations are all that remain. (Courtesy Promised Land State Park.)

In August 1955, hurricanes Connie and Diane struck the northeastern part of the country as 20 inches of rain fell on the area. Ten people died in Greentown alone, and the level of water at the Promised Land Lake dam barely passed under the bridge. Roads and bridges were washed out, and beaches were damaged. Repairs took one year to complete. (Courtesy Carl Rose.)

On May 31, 1998, five tornados swept through the Promised Land region, and one tornado, a category F-2, with winds gusting between 113 and 157 miles per hour, cut through the center of the park. It created a six-mile-long path of damage that was as much as 200 yards wide. This map shows the route of the tornado. (Courtesy Promised Land State Park.)

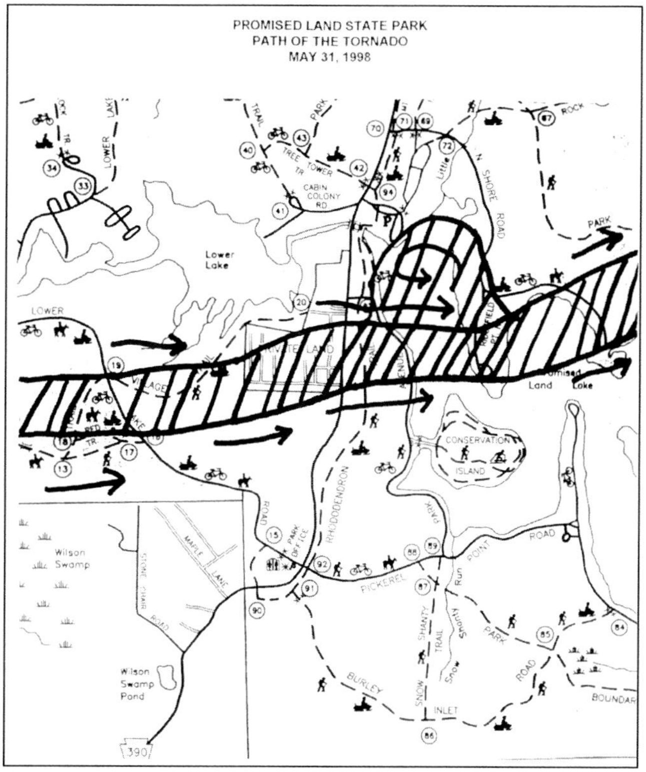

Not since 1955, when hurricanes Connie and Diane passed through, has such damage been seen at the park. Century old trees and utility poles were snapped off, 60 cabins were damaged, and two cabins were destroyed. Park facilities were heavily damaged. The park was cut off from the outside world as efforts were made to open the main arteries of the park and to evacuate the visitors, campers, and cabin owners who were trapped. (Courtesy Promised Land State Park.)

Park personnel; volunteers; local fire, ambulance, and EMT companies; Pennsylvania Power & Light; and Bell Atlantic all assisted in finding hazards, removing stranded patrons, and clearing thousands of downed trees. On June 26, the park, which had been closed for 25 days, reopened and visitors saw a changed landscape, as trees that had stood for decades were now gone along the path of destruction. More than $2 million of damage was done. (Courtesy Promised Land State Park.)

A successful partnership that has been developed over the last 100 years is the cooperative relationship between park volunteers and the professional staff. The volunteers provide untold hours of service to help the park fulfill its mission. Here, the Pike County Snow Runners Snowmobile Club rebuilds the bridge that crosses the spillway on the Promised Land Dam. Volunteers also assist as campground hosts and with cleanups. (Courtesy Promised Land State Park.)

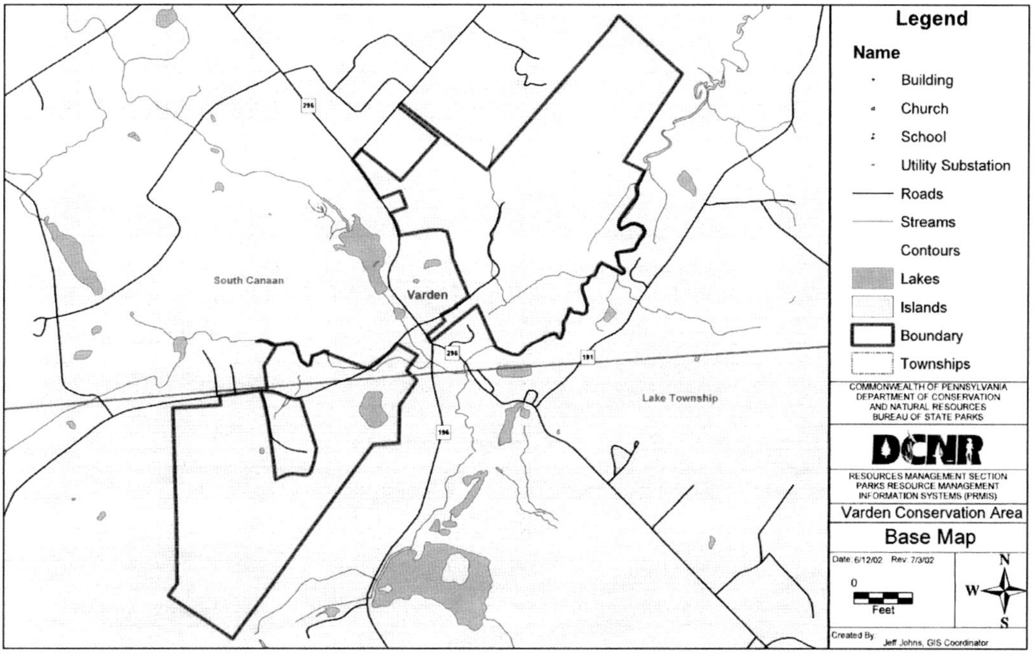

An important national development that is impacting Promised Land is the acquisition of lands not contiguous to the park but that the park units manage. Parks often oversee these properties with other partners. This preserves open space but creates different challenges of administration and funding. The Varden Conservation Area (VCA), a 343-acre tract of undeveloped land near Varden is currently managed by the park. (Courtesy Promised Land State Park.)

The VCA was donated to the commonwealth in 2001 by Dr. Mead Shaffer. The property was once home to a number of farms. This chimney, part of a c. 1790 building , was built by John Shaffer from Montgomery, New York. John Shaffer served in the American Revolution and is an ancestor of Dr. Mead Shaffer. The conservation area will be used for environmental studies and passive outdoor recreation. (Courtesy Geoffrey Gross.)

Precedents were established for the Varden project when Promised Land oversaw the Snow Hill and Peck's Pond State Forest picnic areas and George W. Childs Park in Dingmans Ferry. Childs Park has a deep gorge and three waterfalls, one of which is pictured. Jurisdictions for the picnic areas were returned to the state forest. Childs Park was given to the National Park Service in 1983. (Courtesy Promised Land State Park.)

One of the park's most important missions as it looks to the future is to retain, promote, and preserve its long and interesting history. A number of the leased cabin sites retain their original rustic appearance and architectural significance such as this one. In 1986 and 1987, Whittaker Lodge and the Bear Wallow cabins were listed on the National Register of Historic Places because of their architectural and historical significance. (Courtesy Peter Osborne.)

The park's museum has continued to be improved in the years since its opening. Recently, the park's museum was upgraded again. This time, a major new addition was built onto the existing museum to house the park's natural history collection. The park has proudly opened the newly dedicated Henry E. Masker Park Museum. (Courtesy Ernie Bush.)

Historic artifacts, photographs, documents, CCC memorabilia, and items from the park's natural history collection can all be found in the Masker museum. Thousands of visitors come to the museum each year. The park also owns significant archives related to its history. The museum is managed by park volunteers and is the first and only state park building designed and built exclusively as an environmental museum. (Courtesy David Heiney.)

Henry E. Masker (1899–1992) was a World War I veteran, recipient of the Purple Heart, foreman for the CCC, and a Pennsylvania State Forest Fire Warden for over 60 years. He was married to Margaret Miller Bush (1899–1990), and they were the operators of a boat-and-bait concession at the park and owners of the Mountain Breezes Lodge from 1931 to 1977 and Mountain Breeze Cottages until 1986. The lodge and cottages were located on Shiney Mountain Road. (Courtesy Ernie Bush.)

The construction of the Masker museum and exhibits was made possible by a significant donation from Lynn and Ernie Bush along with a matching grant from BP/Amoco (Ernie's former employer), individual donors, the commonwealth, and the Pennsylvania Parks and Forests Foundation. Here, Gloria Masker Nauman (daughter of Henry Masker), Barbara Davey (center), and Ernie Bush (stepson of Henry Masker) stand with the plaque dedicating the museum to Henry Masker. (Courtesy David Heiney.)

Another significant donation came in 2004, when Tom Frantz (center), a former foreman in the CCC, donated the funding necessary to purchase a bronze statue of a CCC boy that stands outside the museum. Also with him are former park manager Barbara Davey and David Heiney, an active volunteer in the park. It is one of the few memorials in the region that honors the work of the CCC. (Courtesy Promised Land State Park.)

The park has honored its CCC legacy with reunions of CCC enrollees and recognition of their work in the park from 1933 to 1941. The reunions began in 1983, and CCC men and their families have renewed old friendships and created new ones. Park staff and volunteers have been collecting materials for several decades. Promised Land has long maintained the finest collection of CCC memorabilia in the region. (Courtesy David Heiney.)

A number of CCC-era structures from the camp remain, including the blacksmith shop and washhouse (now the park's auditorium). Other structures include a garage, a pump house, and the environmental education office, which was formerly the camp superintendent's office. Evidence of buildings that are long gone remain and can be seen by visitors. (Courtesy Peter Osborne.)

On the day of the CCC reunion, the former blacksmith shop, which was renovated in 1993, is open and living history demonstrations by volunteers are conducted. There are also displays of CCC memorabilia, tools, uniforms, books, and objects used by the CCC boys. Visitors from around the region come to participate in the event. (Courtesy Dave Heiney.)

On June 25, 2005, the park celebrated a century of service. A year-long celebration was commenced to celebrate the park's past and to promote its future. A variety of events were undertaken, including a general park cleanup, tree plantings, historic car shows, lectures, hikes, and live animal presentations. The vision of state park and forest officials beginning in 1898 has essentially been fulfilled. (Courtesy David Heiney.)

One of the most important activities a park can undertake for the future is to plant trees because it reflects hope. It also fulfills one of the missions of the park; to preserve and promote a healthy forest. Here, from left to right, Ernie Bush, Paul Nauman, Rachel Raynie, Alyssa Raynie, Paul "Brud" Nauman, and Anna Raynie plant an American chestnut in honor of the park's centennial. (Courtesy Peter Osborne.)

Another important goal for the future of the park is to create a passion for it with young people. A superb example is Moriah Grace Newnam, who was born in her family's favorite campsite at the park. Newnam was delivered on August 16, 1996, at Pickerel Point Campsite No. 149. Mother Peggy gave birth to her on a Friday evening, and the entire family stayed through the weekend. On another occasion, more than 50 years ago, a family was waiting in line for a prized summer reservation when the mother went into labor. The husband refused to get out of the line. His wife had her baby in the line. (Courtesy David Heiney.)

Families, sometimes following in the footsteps of two, three, four, and even five generations before them, come to the park to refresh their souls. Each comes with a new perspective and a different vision of what the park is, but each knows that it is indeed a special place. Here from left to right, Sandi Corson Naughton, Jackie Herstich, and Angela Affa Master enjoy Promised Land Lake. (Courtesy Promised Land State Park.)

The grand vision of creating parks and forests for the people of Pennsylvania has long endured and continues to guide the park's destiny. As the park looks to its next 100 years, it remains a place that families can visit to enjoy nature and escape from the pressures of modern-day living. Hopefully, that will continue because these are, after all, the people's parks. (Courtesy Herbert Witzenberger.)

BIBLIOGRAPHY

Andrews, Edward. *The People Called Shakers*. New York: Dover Publications, 1963.
Bancroft, Peggy. *This Land of Promise: The Promised Land Story*. A Poconobook Series, 1994.
Blose, Norman. *History of the Promised Land Protestant Community Church*. Greene Township, PA: Promised Land Protestant Community Church, 2002.
Cupper, Dan. *Our Priceless Heritage: Pennsylvania State Parks 1893–1993*. Pennsylvania: Commonwealth of Pennsylvania, Pennsylvania Historical and Museum Commission for Dept. of Environmental Resources, Bureau of State Parks, 1993.
Deubler, Henrietta, Hunter, Margaret, Parke, Nancy. *History of Fairview Lake*. Honesdale, PA: The Printery, 1990.
Forrey, William. *History of Pennsylvania's State Parks*. Harrisburg, PA: Commonwealth of Pennsylvania, Department of Environmental Resources, 1984.
Fluhr, George, ed. *Pike County: Historic Site and Scenic Area Survey*, Pike County, Milford.
"Gold and The Shakers." Shaker Quarterly, Vol. 7, # 1, Spring 1967.
Lehde, Norman. *History of Pike County, Commissioners of Pike County*. Milford, PA: 1989.
"Promised Land State Park, After The Wind Died Down: The Tornado of 1998." Harrisburg, PA: Commonwealth of Pennsylvania, Department of Conservation and Natural Resources, 1998.
"Promised Land State Park Resource Management Plan." Commonwealth of Pennsylvania, Department of Conservation and Natural Resources, August 2004.
"Promised Land Ranger District." Pocono Breeze, Delaware Forest District No. 19, Vol. No. 8, August 1956.
Promised Land State Park: Ancient Rivers and Ages of Ice. Pennsylvania Geological Survey, Bureau of Topographic and Geologic Survey, undated.
Riblett, Wendy Anne. "Environmental & Park News," Park Newsletter, History of Promised Land Park series, A Promised Land Volunteers in Park Publication, 1980s.
Shelton, Sanford. History of Promised Land State Park, in-house documents, 1980 & 1983.

For more information contact the park:

Promised Land State Park
RR 1, Box 96
Greentown, PA 18426
(570) 676-3428